LORGORLIGI LOCOMOTION

A Logologo Collection of Poems

HONDRED PERCENT

MENSA PRESS

MENSA PRESS
9619 Quarry Bridge Court
Columbia, MD 21046

First published in the United States in collaboration with Mensa Press.

US Copyright Number: TXu002252222
ISBN-13: 9798548986689

Printed in the United States of America.

Set in Merchant Ledger Rough Thin and Atlantis Bold Inline fonts
Author photograph by Obed Benyin-Mensah, MD and Kofi Dzogbewu.
Logo design by Foster Toppar Elkharris
Designed by Ras Louis-Sedare Mensch

To my sons, Sean Kwaw Miezah Forjoe AKA BoBo &
Jermaine Paul Kwaw Chi Forjoe.

Some of the poems are accompanied by a Poet's
Note. This is to give you, the reader, a glimpse
into the poet's thought process when those poems
were being created.

TABLE OF CONTENTS

37

Welcome to my 37 station of imagination
Where thoughts gossip and somersault
at the birth of an idea

Summer is laughter

Conversations capture kɔnkɔnsa
and try to give him to a pastor

Ahead of me automobiles blow their
trumpets like rapture
Hawkers follow suit by calling
customers faster

As for me,
I'm writing a chapter

Of poetry lurking around
the city of fractures

The bus stops
The bus blocks
Chale wote goes flip flop

My thoughts hip-hop to tip top melodies
going tick-tock
My thoughts tiptoe to poetry vehicles going
crisscross
The words ziploc, to keep them fresh and not
wish-wash

Which watch, creates words and forms cubicles?
With ideas and verbs to create spoken word
unusual

This poem is strange
but at the same time it's beautiful
Chaos making trends
and also writing a musical

My poems are trotro minibuses
with enthusiasm and flair
My poems krɔ krɔ drivers who flaunt the rules
and don't care

Like a poem parked by the corner
about Abeku
A drivers mate whose only dream,
is to stay cool
Be the hype man for the next superstar so stay
tuned
as he rehearses for his future role like a
cartoon

Oho!

He screams like the wayside preacher
Grabbing everyone's attention
like Ghana must go

I've got poems in the station
about people who show,
who sew kaftans and dresses about people too
known

There are unfinished poems about girls and
their beauty
The kind that radiates and have men asking, "who
is she?"

Who are these emotions pivoting on a better
tomorrow?
A man or pleasure?
Their poems are long and short like letters

I am still trying to understand
the makings of the weather
Like the unfinished piece of Fatima, the pear
seller

9

Whose footsteps massage the ears of the butcher
Dela
Causing his jaw to drop and reminisce about
Fela
Causing his eyes to be transfixed to her
backside

Her back provides, danger like a land slide

But he is stuck like a tracker to a GPS signal
Stuck like a tracker to a GPS signal

There is also the poem of Tata,
the kaayaye street porter
Whose curves got lovers and spouses resetting
their culture
Her curves and tight-fitting clothes are like a
chisel to a potter
Not letting go of money, and admiring Ghana's
daughters

There are visible poems of karma, juju, and love
Poems of Hausa Kooko, and kelewele at night
Poems of sweat, smiles, anger, hate and pleasure
Poems of greed, disease, humility, corruption
and leisure

In my 37 station of imagination,
there are more poems than my eyes can see
Many are drunk on palm wine by the sea
Brewed by disappointment stung by bees

I thus bask in the chaos and confusion
of the people
Watching lines being created and mistakes being
made

By life driving its fingers in the sands as
slaves
Completing and beginning another anthology of
waves

Starting one vehicle,
and parking another

Beginning a journey,
And ending another

And that's how the poems in this station roll
Each is a journey with a story untold

My imagination is a treasure of gold
Filled with many trips for many more roads
For now its late and the station must close
The money you paid will get you home
Maybe tomorrow, I will drive you slow
Taking you places where poetry glows

Bus Stop!

Poet's Notes

Kɔnkɔnsa means gossip in Twi

Krɔ krɔ is a twi term that represents compliments given to get an individual to do something

Ghana Must Go is a popular plastic woven checkered bag with a dark past used by West Africans.

Hausa Koko is a popular Ghanaian porridge (that I am not a fan of)

Kelewele is spiced deep fried ripe plantain chopped into tiny pieces

37 is one of the popular lorry stations of Accra, Ghana. It is also the closest lorry station to the airport in the capital. The station gets its name from the 37 Military Hospital, which is close by. The name 37 is because it was the 37th military hospital to be established by the British in West Africa during the Second World War.

INDEPENDENCE DAY

Independence Day is coming!

So what?

My independence is nothing
My independence is running from success
I can get a bribe for much less
Dependence on corruption has made me file for
contests
That see me paying quite a lot of money for my
lifestyle
Life? Wow!
Tickle me harder so that I can laugh proud
What child?
I father no one but myself
I am a coward
A HIPC nation without a belt
and a lot of tax money
I grow funny like Bugs Bunny
my GDP needs a degree so that I can fill tummies
full,
with nutrients and education,
but things are going the other way
So we need some libation
Akpeteshie will make the gods hear,
as it rises to occasion
but I'm drunk,
so let divorce spare, me
From being separated from independence
I need rehabilitation
Someone, show me the exit

LOCOMOTION

Ghana taxis are mechanical rainbows tattooed
with stickers of hand fists,
Ghana flags, Manchester United, Chelsea,
Barcelona and Liverpool

My liver is cool sipping on hibiscus whilst my
pupils read my daily subscription to Accra's
Readers Digest filled with inspirational
messages on the behinds of taxis and minibuses

Written in English, slang, Pidgin and
vernacular,
these inscriptions paint a scene spectacular
Dumbfound you like a teenager practicing sakawa
Yet make Ghana beautiful like the lady I met
today called Araba

Many of the drivers are unlicensed like African
politicians
They drive malnourished vehicles certified
roadworthy by the system
Which is overloaded like trucks passing through
Spintex and motorway

The state of the country's roads is a motorcade
of disappointment
A visual representation of our path to success
flooded by potholes and speed ramps
Potholes created by corruption, and speed ramps
created by greed to enable seeds collect in
this oware board made of tar and gravel

But the game is tilted to those in power
Enabling the nations vehicle to not reach its
destination
We are stuck on a roundabout that has no exits
A crossroads that keeps spinning, confusing us
of our direction

14

Mechanical flags called traffic lights boldly
decorate and flash our national colors as a
symbol of patriotism
Or is it nepotism?
A twisted tourism that showcases our disregard
for order
Allows motorcycles to cross red lights,
and motorcades assist those with the means
to run around town like they are the President

As I speak, many of these lights are
malfunctional, requiring the assistance of
traffic officers dressed in
black and white with white gloves whose job
reminds us not of order, but instead,
segregation and the King of Pop,
Michael Jackson

By day, these police officers of the law collect
fines for traffic violations which
miraculously turn to bribes
They evolve into toll officers and hawkers by
night
Legally wiring money from drivers and
pedestrians alike into their personal bank
accounts
It's a roundabout flooded by indiscipline and
immorality with no U-turn in sight

Black or white?
This is the question posed by these officers
Posed unconsciously, even to themselves

I swell in the thought process of ethical
social issues
With engines running, as well as tissues,
into the chuku chaka nature
of our transport system

Revealing to us, not only the ignorant nature of
drivers, but rather,

that both the car and driver
the nation is using to reach its destination

Need to be changed

Poet's Notes

Sakawa is a Hausa word which means inserting or making money. In recent times it has become the Ghanaian term for illegal activities performed on the internet to make money. It sometimes involves traditional rituals to improve the success rate of the scams. "Chuku Chaka" is the name Ghanaians have attached to the sound of trains as they move. Chaka however, represents chaos, dirty or mess.

These two words are interesting as they seem to possess dual meanings. This is similar to the title of the piece which can be interpreted as motion or, Loco-motion (crazy movements). Are we going forward, backward or sideways?

A TALE OF TWO COMPANIES

There are two companies situated around the
Cantonments' roundabout

One is a majority male only limited liability
company

The other,

a female only NGO

Her engines blows and screws like a factory
Her product is better than satisfactory
She is underrated as a business for she works
the night scene

A night queen hidden in the day getting in the
way of men
Begging them to give away their cash and a
little more

Bank managers visit the office often
So do pensioners and expatriates
She always on time and never late

Elevates her makeup

Customer service is needed if you are going to
get the price to shoot up

It often does

Her marketing has the effect of selling drugs

Tax is evaded, meanwhile the value is emanated
in the structure of this company

They pride themselves in encrypted
transactions, and have no links to crypto
They prefer fashion that has zip codes,

and cause their feet to tip toe

But where is the tipping point?

Constant attempts have been made
to pull down the company and take it away from
the free zone

The annual reports, however, show that the
business is lucrative

Better than a day job they say,
better than a day job they claim,
I guess, this NGO is here to stay

The limited liability company sees more than
the government, has more news than the press,
and a mix of things just like a pot of palm nut
soup

Good and evil, a bunch of julor in uniforms and
legitimate heroes

In real life they are bad, but in the movies,
they are heroes

Sometimes they are villains with superpowers,
who bribe with a tower of authority

The kryptonite to this fraternity of super men
is corruption

So traffic violations swiftly turn into
hypocrisy

Is it protect and serve?
Or protect the deserved? Or revered?
I better put on weight
and get a pot belly to deter
Sergeant Bediako for taking the beggars
5 GHC to repair,

his credit line at the drinking spot next door

Limited in power, liable to the law
Autobots turned Decepticons, see how they
transform

Some good, some evil
Their uniform could be your sequel
to the worst day in your life
Like a bad guy meeting Steven Segal

The two companies share the same land
A land home to the lavish and well off
The irony is well caught
It's not far from a school which is rumored to
be well taught

They see each other working in the good and the
bad

I think a merger is in order
For their turnover, to be mad

Poet's Notes

*From about 9PM in the evening in Accra, Ghana,
you will find women dressed up hanging around
the Cantonments round about and roads leading
to it. In my early days I found it weird but
later realized they were prostitutes.
Their sister company, the police, usually set up
a stop around the Togo Embassy close by.*

*One would think the presence of the police will
deter these women from their trade, but it
doesn't. I used to marvel at how these two
opposites exist in a prestigious neighborhood
like Cantonments in the evening each time I
went home.*

*I also wondered, who made more money between the
two companies.*

GOD DEY

God dey before man dey
Sun dey before Moon dey
Somedays we go hungry
But hungry, is a luxury
Cos hunger leads to anger
And anger creates thunder
But for thunder to thunder
Lightning, for answer
That answer be power
En wey e dey under
The cover of hunger
So hunger, be power
If man no make hungry
He no go pray humbly
So hungry is bluntly
Seasoned discovery
Of God and his power
To heal and to shower
When hungry, don't cower
Just pray and discover
That God dey,
Monday,
Tuesday to Sunday
When things come make someway
Remember that God Dey

I DON'T LIKE THIS PLAY

Act I

The stage is set in a time where the air that
gives us life has been poisoned
Poisoned by a warlord that is no respecter of
class, race or country
Yet, this is not the reason we are dying
We die from a fire that begun by us collecting
firewood
We understood that peace hated squabbles
So we quarreled with our stubbornness
The friction gave birth to a fire that got
tired of the arguing
It got tired and changed from a friend that
brought warmth, to the grim reaper
We're grim speakers, pouring fuel onto this fire
by fighting passionately amongst ourselves on
issues of race,
black lives matter, and rape
As if our attacks on each other aid in
defeating the common enemy

The air before this war was already poisoned by
our greed and polluted by selfishness
Despite the many warnings of future doom
We continued to suffocate
Suffocate ourselves with a blanket of smoke
claiming ignorance as the cause
I wish I could fault smoke as the cause of this
new reality
However, for smoke to rise, a fire must be lit
The earth seems to have been spared by the evil
war Lord
I wonder whether she channeled some of her
prayers his way for mercy to ease the pressure
Ease the pressure of the knee that society has
on the neck of the environment screaming,
"I-can't-breathe"

Act II

The venomous warlord is the protagonist and
enemy in this tragic epic that I do not like
An invisible war is being fought
We know not whether we are retreating or
charging forward
We are at a loss on how to defeat the enemy
The bio warfare used by our foe is a complex
strategy we and our sages are yet to comprehend

It has caused children to play indoors and
politics to play outside
Schools are closed
Loneliness is open for an open relationship
with society
Bedrooms turn to mosques and churches,
forcing members to test their faith in their
homes

In the absence of integrity,
the warlord calls for masks to be worn by all
characters for protection
Further complicating the identification
process

In masking ourselves,
we mask our emotions and unmask commotion
Further complicating our ability to see the
pain and effect of the war on our souls

Act III

The play I don't like progresses
It details the lives of individuals
It details their losses, death of loved ones,
innovations and increased attention to the
statistics of the war
Amid the confusion and tragedy,
I am stuck in sadness on one issue too simple
and painful for me to deal with

I am stuck and mad, that no one else can see
that something is missing
This something, is not the cure to the war,
or weapon one can use in ending our enemy

It's not a vaccine

In a play of masks and tragedy,
I sit as a character and member of the audience

Mystified

Mystified by the nature of the war

In my bad space,
I light a cigarette of thoughts to smoke my
questions
Hoping, that the war, the air, or the poison,
will have an answer to this bad play

Have an answer to my simple question:

"How can I tell, if someone in a mask, is
smiling?"

The End

Poet's Notes

I remember the first couple of times I went out with a mask after the Covid lockdown. It was strange. The first thing that hit me was how I could not tell whether people were smiling. It felt as if this was an opportunity for many to not smile. For me it was a difficult process to tell someone a heartfelt "hello". This is what inspired the poem.

The line with the knee is in reference to the George Floyd murder. I guess we all get a faint idea of how it feels to be oppressed. This time however, we are being oppressed by a virus.

Maybe I am wrong

I FELL

I fell, she said
Slipped on a banana peel whilst walking to
church, she said

That?

Oh, that is just marks from a belt
for weight loss
I accidentally cut myself with broken,
lip-gloss

Rick Ross's CD was playing,
and I was dancing to it
Next thing I see,
I was just flying, through it

Glass

Three pieces were stuck in my ass
Whoever said hip-hop was dangerous
surely, did not mean the dance

I put bandages on my hands just to feel cool
The other time it was because I slipped whilst
cleaning the pool

Speaking of cool,
I've got about twenty pairs of shades
Five of different colors, one for each day

He said I look nice
when I wear shades in the day
He said it kind of makes me look
like a celeb' in a way

For some strange reason I feel cold,
that is why I wear jackets
That?
That is from when I was young,

my brother hit me with a racket

Except that she had no brother

Vanessa was an only child
Who was raped at seven
by a man who was Holy

Now, he is best friends with the Reverend
She got raped again at eleven
Eleven years later she was married to a guy,
named Kevin

And,
she did not slip on a banana peel
Rather, she was hit with a banana peel
Followed by a fist that hit her face,
and made her body kneel

There was no arrest appealed,
but her body hit the floor,
and we saw those marks
Trust me, they were not from weight loss

They were from an umbrella,
in response to a question by Vanessa

"Why are you coming home late?"

And the umbrella smashed the cake - and the lip-
gloss,
which explains, the cuts she got on her face

She said, "I was dancing to Rick Ross"
Kevin did not like the moves I was making
Next thing I'm flying through glass,
with my ass cut, in three places

That is why I had the bandages
and the Ray Ban glasses,
and four other designer pairs

that I wore in between classes

It gave me self-confidence

I told her to tell an audience or the police,
but she said,
"Brother, I do not have the self-confidence!"

This was all a week ago
Wish I had known she was lying,
known she had been crying,
denying that man was at fault

She said,

"It is my fault"

Indeed, the fault is mine
Now I recite her story hoping,
whoever hears,
will stop the crime

Poet's Notes

This poem is inspired by an advert I saw in South Africa in my college days (Somewhere between 2005-2010) about domestic violence. It spoke about the invisible nature of the offence.

There was a girl in college who dated a guy who used to beat her up. When it was mentioned to me, it was hard for me to believe that it was real. After all, what does a woman beater look like? It made me realize that the crime was closer to home than I cared to realize.

I wrote the poem to speak out against the act and to reveal its mastery of invisibility. Just because we don't see it doesn't mean it's not happening. Let's speak out against domestic violence.

AGAMA

There is a rap that the lizard spits
A rap the lizard spits to get its tongue to
twist and shift the mists
Shift the bliss, the truth, the proof and hide
the miss
Hide the piss, hide the foul coming out of the
pits
Coming out of the fits, of chaos dancing adowa
to the djembe that decided to play a hip-hop
beat to this dead-beat reptile spitting lines

There is a rap that the lizard spits that gets
the women to swing their hips
A rap that gets their seas to rock the ships,
rock the bones, rock the tits
Sending these vessels into the palms of the
people, but there is a slip
A blip, redirecting the cargo to different
destinations like a flip

There is a rap that the lizard spits
A rap that gets their wits to be aroused by his
slick, his lick, his flick,
of flow and rhyme designed to create sensation,
but not brick
To cement together to create a castle of impact,
no, this is a trick

The lizard spits a rhyme that is sick
A line so attractive infecting his audience
into thinking they're rich
They are pricked with promises of a better
tomorrow by a penis that is thick
Thick of AIDS and a profane lifestyle covered
by a condom that is dripped, ribbed,
Stripped of its protection by a hole that is
ticked
Ticked for destruction, to allow hypocrisy to
flow like the bars that he picks

The lizard is a hustler
A cold-blooded gangster claiming to be a
businessman, but he is a pimp
Pimping our future into a brothel and a chick,
hungry for cocks
to provide sustenance or a quick,
Escape from the madness brought about by the
BIC

There is a rap that the lizard spits
A rap that sheds his skin to print sacrifice on
his smile and sin
An act to sway the crowd like gin
Into being merry and accept this reptile
as a pin
On the hearts of the people,
but beware the grin
The grin of deception, that grows back within
Hiding in labor, the other side the twin

There is a rap that the lizard spits
A rap of politics, poli-tricks and spit
bumps his head to the streets, to the power, to
the sweet,
fragrance of opportunity, that abounds in the
weak, and the addiction to the crack, that he
spews with his beat

There is a rap that the lizard spits
I remember it not 'cos I'm reminded of the
thought, of the lizard when he last bought, the
ignorance of the people
He bought their ignorance at the evil, market of
elections, patronized by the feeble
It was there he rapped me his greatest crime,

"Just because the agama lizard bumps its head to
hip-hop,
doesn't mean,

it likes the beat"

THE WORLD'S LYRICS

They say when you are happy,
you enjoy the music
When you are sad, you listen to the lyrics
I guess,
I am listening to the lyrics right now

It says I should follow my dreams,
but my dreams turned into nightmares
I am speaking to deaf people,
listening to dumb guys
I am seeing thumbs cry,
with their faces painted in ink
The clouds here are black
Our vehicle for life has gone off track
And I see the prophecy of doom,
clearly in the rain

You see, until we realize that our morals are
infected
That our own people profited off slavery
Sold their people as commodities
Saw it as an opportunity, business, necessary, a
reason for war
Until we understand the irony of the symbols of
unity such as kente
The contrast in the physical
That our way of life now is no different than
that of our forefathers
Until we open our eyes to the disunity that
exists
Dissolve politics, party lines,
tribes, religion and culture
I am afraid, we will still be here talking over
each other's heads

Until we stop seeing women as sexual objects
Realize the royalty and superiority within them
Treasure their contribution to life

33

Make more than an effort to recalibrate society
on consent, the norms of life
Until we realize that the length of a skirt has
nothing to do with rape
Neither is it an invitation for sexual
misconduct
Until this happens,
I am afraid, we will still be here talking over
each other's heads

You see, we live in a world where love is an
eclipse
A rare occurrence that appears as magic or
miracle until some scientists explains the
physics

But love is not an eclipse

It's a unicorn that only a few see
A unicorn with wings to fly when the world
tells it to hide because its cold outside

We live in a world that believes
BIG is better
So we look down on the little things in life and
fill ourselves with lies so that those around
look smaller

So we hate our siblings

We create a world where mothers kill their
children and husbands their wives
We live in a world where robbery occurs in
broad daylight
People rob others not of their phones,
but of their body parts

We live in a world where mothers are fathers
and fathers, mothers
Where men don't understand women, and women don't
understand men

We live in a world where pastors abuse their
congregation, and the congregation see it as a
blessing
A world where the occupants are at war with the
land they live on
A world where greed fuels ambition
Where both adults and children lack discipline

I feel discipline nowadays is like fast food
with democracy as the takeaway package
Yet the only thing taken away,
is the opportunity to raise a generation fit to
survive in this storm of immorality

The angry Ghanaian is dead
Along the road from slavery to colonization,
independence and coup d'etats
Disappointment hired an assassin to murder the
angry Ghanaian

There was a time when angry was good
Not wrong
It united us and gave us purpose
Angry proved we were human
Without it, we fail to truly live

They say when you are happy,
you enjoy the music
When you are sad, you listen to the lyrics

I do not know whether I am happy or sad

For I stopped enjoying the music
I stopped listening to the lyrics
of society long ago

I stopped dancing to the tunes
I stopped studying the words

Now I follow the birds
Earnestly seeking the music they sing

Listening to their lyrics of freedom to gain
inspiration

And maybe,
just maybe

I will begin … to write a song

TICKLE

When the world tickles my mind

I do not laugh

My funny bone is missing
My eye keeps twitching

I think a while back I was short sighted

Now, I'm long sighted
Not delighted with the change in frame and
lenses
I would prefer to speak in past tenses
Because nowadays we pass sentence without
realizing that it ends with a warning

A full stop

Fool, STOP!

Stop, with your hypocritical nonsense!

This coupled with a lack of moral self-control
got my mind tickled but,

I'm not laughing

I'm not laughing, but gasping for air and
surprised to find it
For I feel that the air is also disgusted with
the life it is serving

How do parents cut a child's fingers?
Prostitute their kids for cybersex?
How do people stand trial with the possibility
to face death because they are suspected of
being gay?
When was two billion dollars not enough to tend
to the needs of people?

We live carelessly

Our toys of luxury are literally
driving us to death

Instead of our Governments taking a nationwide
stand to abandon the use
of fossil fuels,
they are still encouraging it

In the past, China's air was so polluted from
gases emitted from factories and cars that
workers had to wear masks
Children had to be indoors

In 2020, we wear masks not to protect ourselves
from gases but the Corona Virus
The situation is truly ironic

Halloween is happening too early
and seems to be lasting more than a day
Taking health instead of candy

It's a funny world but no one is laughing
Too much material for standup comics
Same material can make a sensitive person vomit
A politician omit,
action to protect the environment and the poor

No one is asking how we can stop it

Even if we ask,

the answer won't change a thing
For we enjoy the filth we live in
We are so comfortable with our obsession with
social media and the internet that our phones
and devices are now our new homes

Earth is just a place we exist to utilize these
facilities

So yes, I am tickled

I am tickled by tragedy and madness

But you will hear no laughter

You will see no smile

For all this tickling does,
is turn my life,

into a joke...of pain

SLOW SIN

I want to be a slower sinner
Start telling the truth, make my lies thinner
I want to be the winner,
of the lowest sins committed on earth
and I want that prize to be given at dinner

My head is getting bigger
So I try to remove ego and try out
to be a singer

"I don't have a big ego"

That will be a hit in the winter

It will be on the billboard,
and I will have a six figure

At that point, I'll definitely be a giver

Because I'm richer
I'll give my money to charity quicker

I'll give my money to charity?
Quicker?

Sin is catching up fast
Will it last?
I've got to get off this righteous path
It's filling me up fast
I must give off gas
But...I shall pass

Because hypocrisy stinks
Reminds me of dirty sinks
We've had too much to drink
The communion glass is empty
We have drunk too much to think!

Wink! Wink! Think! Think!

Before your eyes go blink, blink!
You can't tell which one is real,
it's a problem, rethink!
Like Louis Vuitton and Gucci bags
Imitated with groovy tags
Just like Christians
Imitators with groupie tags
Pastors in a groovy pad
Please reconsider pursue rehab

We have sold our minds to self-righteous signs
which are fake,
but you can only tell if your soul is refined

Mankind Christians, foot soldiers for hells
business
Judging who is going to hell and who is not
They're the witness
Going to church in fashion, pretending they
have passion
I step back and ask, "is Christianity high
fashion?"

Eye catching? Let's be real
Cut the crap and conceal
The hate inside and feel
The love we need to heal

So I want to be a slower sinner
I'll start telling the truth, but my lies may not
be thinner
I am really a beginner
I recognize Christ as the winner
Hopefully one day, I'll sit with him at dinner

All this considered,
I still want to be a singer
Act in a blockbuster, and not be the killer

My head may be getting bigger
But whose head doesn't? Go figure

I may not be richer,
but I'll never be a quitter
I'll try to give an offering,
pay my tithe quicker

Hopefully with all this,
I'll be a slower sinner
Encourage others, pray,
and hope for God, to deliver

JESUS'S BROTHER

He was always better
Nothing I did could compare
Mother was always on my case,

"Why can't you be like your big brother?"

I mean, how can you beat walking on water?
Even Peter couldn't walk ten steps
Sorry, I didn't introduce myself
My name is...

Is it even necessary?

My name was never really mentioned
Only my existence along with my other siblings

You might as well call me, Jesus's brother

I know, I know, I should be using my real name

But honestly,
you are more likely to hear my story with my big
brother's name attached

J, yeah, that was what I called him

I didn't believe at first you know
Not about him being a stepbrother,
that was pretty obvious

He looked nothing like the rest of us
His hair was so perfect, face never saw a
pimple
Even had our sisters saying,

"I wish I could be beautiful like Jesus"

I sometimes thought that he was gay

I mean, girls were always saying he was
beautiful, and he was always on about love, even
to guys!

What was I to think?

I feel bad though
You see, I used to tease him in school with my
friends

Dumb thing, right?

Never in front of him though

It didn't last long
Because one day he sat me down and told me word
for word,
everything my friends and I had said

You can imagine the stupid look on my face?
The scary part was that he was not even angry
He actually said I was creative with my insults
But should put my creativity to better use
That's J for you my friends

As I was saying, I didn't believe at first
That he was going to die for us and all
I mean, I was like his number one fan
I saw the miracles firsthand
I even performed some of them
But not like his

His were masterpieces!

I will never comprehend how we fed all those
people with few loaves and fish
TWICE!

It's not as if extra kept being sneaked in

I mean, we were on a hill for crying out loud

44

No bakery or fish market for another 500 miles
The bread just kept being broken and everyone
one was fed, with extra left
That's J

Such a cool feeling

Same feeling got me hooked up with my wife

I just had to say,

"Hey there, Jesus is my big brother"

That was it!

Jesus blessed the marriage

I must say, it's good to have spiritual
connections

Never took his death well though

J is just too nice
I mean, this brother who raised the dead and
chased out demons had to be whipped like that?

No man!
That was wrong!
He did nothing wrong
His only crime was being born on this bloody
planet called earth
It tore me up I tell you

It's not as if he was not strong,
or couldn't fight
I mean, we would play wrestle and fight as kids
for sport
Never once did I win
He was strong
You had to be if you were a carpenter those days

Besides, he had read so much from the temples
that he knew about battle in and out

Jesus, my big brother!
Forgive he always said
Even when they tie you up to a cross?

You should have seen mother
She cried her heart out for you
It was not easy, but you had it worse
What a guy

Three days after, you rose up

My MAN!

Had the chance to speak to you
You broke it down for me how you tore hell up
I see all the training in the gym was to break
down the gates of hell to free us

Patience is a virtue
Would have loved for you to stay longer,
but you said Pops had a job for you

It was a sad and happy time saying goodbye
Especially when you flew, rose, flew?

Me and the wife are still arguing over that
Please give the answer to the person you are
sending down to help us

This is a tribute to you
I used my creativity to praise you

I hope I did good by you

I may not be remembered for my name

I don't mind

I am just proud to be called,

Jesus's Brother

Poet's Notes

*This poem was written in 2011 from a challenge
posted by Poetra Asantewa in the People Of
Equal Thoughts and Spirit (POETS) group titled
'Religious Personas'.*

*We were to take a Biblical character or event
and write a poem on it in a different setting or
context.*

*Now when I look back, I try to imagine where
creativity would take me with this task with
what I know now. I would probably write about
how Jesus was a Ghanaian who belonged to the
Ewe tribe. His father after all was a carpenter.*

I'M NOT A POET

I am not a poet
I am just passing through
My passion flew past academics and all I was
trying to do
Was to get Dzifa's lips to widen to,
a curve of mathematical nature,
but my mathematical data fails me
For when Mr. Mensah lectured on trigonometry,
I was calculating why you were ignoring me

Mtchewwwww

That was your answer to my compliments
You ruptured my confidence

My similes I believe were infected with disease
So even though it spelt, "I smile"
My enemies were the ones it pleased
But not you

I am not a poet,
but I had to try
Dzifa was looking for that kind of guy
But I was kind of shy
I was kind of,
not experienced in the "hey" and the "hi"
I was more of the, "bye-bye" every time I got
close to expressing my feelings
But I had to try

You see you expected me to speak English
But instead, I spoke love

My accent was my body language
You liked the way I brofolized my hug
My chale wote lacked finesse but eased tension
Made you relax for my in-tention
I'm a dada b repenting from his wannabe ways,

applying for a job in your heart and at the same
time,

Expecting a raise

It's not bragging if it's the truth, but this
is...roshing

For the rush that I feel
that you feel that we feel,
makes us dangerous armed robbers
without ski masks

Killing time and robbing each other of sadness
It's so good, it turns a bit into madness

Where did you come from?

For I don't know what to do with these lines in
my head except draw them around you

But the lines turn to curves, and you became a
sinner
For your hip game is sin, I mean sine curves
My mathematics is a bit weird
Our algebra is a bit blurred, for we don't want
to find Y,

and we don't want to be exes

Life is good right now,
but we don't want to be Nexus
We want to...
Google each other every day until we become the
Apple of our eyes

And I am not a poet,
I am just passing by
But if this drive by down poetry lane captures
your heart

Then I'll pass by more often,
to leave you with a smile

Poet's Notes

This poem is being used as the second track in my upcoming album titled B.O.R.E (Book Of Rhymes Exquisite). It takes the form of rap; however, I feel when it is released you will appreciate the dual nature of this piece as rap as well as poetry.

LONELY

Is she the most beautiful girl I have ever
seen? No
But who is keeping score?
How can I ignore her contours,
Shai Hills, spills of Dulux paint
in the perfect colour of Cappuccino candy
number 2?

You…look…gorgeous? No

Alright is more like it

You see I know Gorgeous
She isn't here right now
so I'll settle for you

You who is …

How can I put this nicely without hurting her
feelings?

You who is everything, but not her

You incurred a loss by stumbling, falling
Ensuring that my appalling disregard for your
looks drives you crazy like Monday mornings

Wanting more and more, of…me

She loved the idea
I didn't care about the idea
I didn't create the idea
I stumbled on the idea
Because I feared, being lonely

Holy doesn't come around much when man is
lonely!
As I said before, I know Gorgeous
But she ain't around now, so I'll settle for you

Like I settle for Coke when Coke Light is not
available
Like I settle for GTV when DSTV is not
available
Like swimming pools when the sea is not
available

You don't know it; but you tempt me

Mend the emptiness that exists
because she Gorgeous can't be around right now

You see that crown you'll never wear
You can rock my body to the night air
In a fashion that will make you realize that I'm
unfair

Because I already got a Queen of my heart
You were staring at a poker face that got you
'gaga
You enjoyed my 'lala
I don't laugh "ha-ha"
but definitely say "ta-ta"

Before I knew it she unzipped herself and
proceeded in my direction

Every swing she makes in those jeans signify
genuine hip melodies

She's tempting me without knowing she could be
the end of me

You see I'm attracted to IT not her

Is it fair, that I am moved by her purr?

I incur unjustified emotions
She is a weird love potion

Gorgeous, can your love potion prevent me from
indulging in she who is just visiting my ocean?

It's confusing because I love you
But I like IT

You have IT, but your IT,
you see your…IT is not here
I want your IT here because, she's here

She has an IT

Not quite the IT I'm used to but…
an IT just the same

Different frame, name, fame?

I'm not sure about that Gorgeous
But if you close from work come home quickly

Come home quickly and find me
For I need you close

or else, I'll overdose

IT TAKES TWO TO TANGO

I hear it takes two to Tango
You need two to make things work

I hear it takes two to Tango
Two to make love work?

Tell me this then

How does a single cell organism like an amoeba
make love to itself?

A-sexually it screws itself with passion

Without a one-night stand or hand
No why didn't you call?
You left your draws, I am involved with another,
I have to go, my mother is about to call?

Yes! Yes! Yes!

A-sexually it screws itself without a one-night
stand

So on this one night I stand,
a single cell lover
A prostitute and casanova cocktail in a locker
Sipping on my own deadly mix of love

I shall booze on this love
Pass out on it with Kamasutra till the morning
comes in a spray
This is not gay or straight,
I state,
I am sick of women turning down this face

This phase of I am a good guy is over,
I am now in a Range Rover
The air conditioner is on
So I am now a cold face with a shoulder

High!

Because I don't give a damn!
If you are a ma-dam, diva, midnight fever,
temptation healer, stealer of sadness and fear

I fear, you have lost me, to myself

My health shall never stutter
in highs and lows
For you are now a long ago
I am a go
You are a …
Stop, wait, listen to me make love to myself as I
walk
and I am loving it

No masturbation
Just a creation of love for oneself to feel
good

It takes…two to tango
It takes…two to tango,
two to get tangled,
two to lose their bangles,
two to strangle,
two to manhandle the relationship,
this nation is sick,
with something bigger than malaria

Baby! Sit STILL!

As I will my heart to be healed
I needed shield from this pain, insane, profane,
game, I need to maintain!
My swagger

Not for you, you, you or you but myself

My very, fly looking self

It takes two to tango

I lead you follow
You follow at an angle
This dance is crooked,
we will never reach the finals
Even Beauty and the Beast danced better
I am now an idle lover

It takes two to tango
Well, screw the dance teacher
For I'm alone in this fiasco

Poet's Notes

*This poem is the aftermath of a painful breakup.
I remember writing this poem during a poetry
event by MadaGhana aka Crystal Tettey at
Highgate hotel in North Ridge in 2011. Something
about one of her poems sparked this train of
thought of anger. A breakup can write beautiful
poetry*

I STOLE YOUR HEART

I stole your heart in a way that is insane that
makes men say that we are engaged, but we are in
play

Play mummy and daddy or house
every single day

Play house as parents with no kids in the way

To make us pay school fees like everyday

It's not because I don't want kids with you but,
hey

I think we'll make more kids than we can pay

For we skip right to the bedroom every time we
play

So we must wear protection every time we
take, ourselves to the next level

We should be careful not to make the earth
tremble

I've been here before, but I don't think this was
the venue

Plus I was with a different girl
I don't know if I should tell you

I do what I do
But I don't like what I'm doing
I am into you girl
I don't understand why I'm fooling
I kiss five girls a week, but you are the first
to influence
My thought process for being monogamous

Please get me through this Decepticon
lifestyle
Playing with these girls' heads deceiving them
in deceptive ways conning their life out

Time out

30 heart breaks can pan out, for a record
But where is my award for this lifestyle?

Killing girls with kisses
Pretending that they're the missus
Kissing them in the missus room with a camera
to revisit

The missus misses the visit
Though evidence is vivid
Lingerie in the bedroom

How could she miss it?

She didn't
I didn't
Deny that it wasn't hers

What I said instead
is that I wanted her to play nurse

I stripped wore the lingerie
Told her to operate, turn me straight
Twisted the story around, go meditate

But she found out eventually

Girl was tired of playing nurse
Sick thing is I didn't care that she hurt
The question is,
was she worth...it?

Probably not

But can I look at you and say that you are not?

I don't want to hurt you
So baby give me a curfew
I don't want my actions to cause tears to work
you
Let's take things slow
Let our lips suck words to serve you
Let's hang passion back on the tree to bear
fruit

Let me not hurt you
Let me not scare you
Play nurse for real, heal me
Make me resentful
Of my past life
Of my past strife
To enjoy the passion fruit,
with my last wife

RECESSION

Currently unemployed in the relationship
sector
My boss said, I do not give enough pleasure
My interest rate in her dropped to a mere zero
My share price increased, I was every female's
hero

Therefore, I looked through my stock exchanges
Searching for a new girl that I can relate with
Mind over money, money over mind
I bought into this chick that had a big behind

Checked her balance sheet, she had liabilities
big as her breasts they offered me the
opportunity
To view her fixed assets, lingerie in her closet
Trust me, the warehouse was full of stock

I could have knocked on other doors but, hers
was unlocked
With the option of getting your money back if
you were not, satisfied
Me, I was gratified
Hung in the air, like a flipping satellite
So surprised she was not listed on the JSE

Johannesburg must be tripping

I took her to the bergs for some sipping,
kissing,
Realized I was missing
A few zero digits
My account must be slipping
Into this girl's bra, pin code in her arms
You have to admit I was liquidated in style

She Nam One'd me
Saw the Gold and not the Ponzi
Need Herbal Life to the Max to get comfy

With 100 Ghana to my name
I stormed into this bar called Clay
Ordered two shots of alomo to drink my sorrows
away
Thank God they had a standard and charted a
taxi my way
Kofi Kinata's Confessions was all I could play

But I was looking for love in the wrong places
Kissed the wrong faces
I lost a good girl 'cos I pissed her off in the
right places
Now I try to look for good girls in wrong spaces
Making love complicated by chasing the wrong
chases

Cal warned me about banking all hopes on love
I should have banked on capital
The security on that is magical
Complicated Fidelity only promised short term
feelings
But not like lust which caught me 7 days later

I met this sweet girl at Zenith
She asked for credit
Girl was so fine, I had to debit
The opportunity cost of that gal was set
I'm an opportunist, I had seen no losses yet
She took me to Republic; bought me a drink
Whispered that I should repay her in kindness I
think
She could tell I was horny, ordered an Uber our
way
I was drunk, offered to pay using Express Pay
The Uber was fake, the sticker spelt u-b-a
It was a scam
Hey, but what was I going to say
I was gone, drunk of lust to tell
Was robbed at gunpoint
Debited and broke as hell

This opportunity cost me my wallet and cards
For I was trying to buy love with credit and
drinks at bars

Her pimp was the shareholder
The dividend his pay
This is more than an economics lesson I say

I succumbed to lust's offer
Was left without coin in my locker
Was looking for love the wrong way so,
ma bor ka

The flesh is weak from Monday to Sunday
I need God to come and save me in Bentley

I was devalued
Argued with my self-values
I realized I valued sex more than I did my boo

Therefore, I called you
Asked If I could come through
Chew on my pride
Spit out a brand new

Cheque of love
One billion sweet kisses
Sweet dishes of love and trust spread with a
dozen six wishes

It seems wicked
That life would play with my heart like cricket
Until I realized that I had crushed my wicket

Yes, it seems livid
For I have come to a conclusion
I had to face a recession before I could come to
your music

It seems livid

But I have come to a conclusion
I had to face a recession before I could come to
your,

music

Poet's Notes

*The inspiration for this poem is from a witty
poem on alcohol and hair products from friend
of mine in South Africa. I heard it and decided
to do something similar using banks and
financial references. How many of these
references do you recognize? There are 7
Ghanaian banks in this and one of them is no
more.*

*This poem has also been selected to feature in
the upcoming B.O.R.E album.*

FRIEND ZONE

Dear Princess,
I know that's not your name
I can't find another word that describes your
perfect ways

You're different

Your speech is so insane
Every time I hear your voice,
I swear I can't contain, my emotions

You didn't know about them
All you knew was that I was a friend and I cared
about you regardless of your weight or taste

Girl, give me a break

Don't pretend you do not understand these
feelings that I make

It is evident,
Sherlock Holmes is not needed in this residence

Even Ghana Police can solve this without
corrupting their intelligence

Sorry,

I know your dad is an officer,

but I want us to get together even though I'm
not popular

Popular belief states,

best friends when put together, make more money
than which is won in the sweepstakes

You can check my briefcase

Filled with love letters written to you from
the 21st of January to my release date

When is that?

I was hoping your heart could tell me

Ever since I left the friend zone it's been hard
for me to tell the, state of affairs within you
Mine was to share, but I feared I'll blow my
chance and you'll not want me to interfere with
your love triangles

I was hoping we could be diagonal
I can calculate math, but I cannot calculate
your phenomenal
Beauty merged with those two B's, 32's
and my success rate if I should pursue thee

Let me rule out calculus

Let us just say you are fabulous

They say a kiss will tell if we are meant to be
monogamous

So kiss and tell

Some say my lips is a wishing well
So wish for love
I'll break your hearts Da Vinci code with my
cells wireless

You are a model on project runway
Sometimes I get the feeling that this loving is
just one way

Is it?

At this point I don't care

I just wish that after this kiss you'll learn to
call me dear

Is it fair that I am knee deep in your
poetry and you notice me
drowning in your essence yet you stare without
holding me to your heart?

Let my kiss be your guide in part
Let me show you tonight,
that I'm your knight in the dark

Poet's Notes

I have been friend zoned a couple of times in my
lifetime. In fact, I was friend zoned by my wife
before we got together. I am not sure whether
it's a testing area for ladies to determine
whether a man is worth the trouble. I believe
the zone has a door to exit. Its however an exit
many guys struggle to use. I guess being in the
friend zone sometimes feels better than
acknowledging that the love conquest is a
failure.

SAVANNAH FLIRTING

Our eyes did more than connect

They had picnics in Serengeti overlooking Zebra
migrating to Nairobi

My pupils chose the location and the goosebumps
on your neck whispered,
"you know me"

We only live once

And yet this gaze has broken up with lonely

And with all this intimacy
that we can endure forever

All I wanted, was your phone number

Our picnics revealed more than attraction

It opened a homework of math equations itching
for division and subtraction

A subtraction of reality to allow this game of
ampe we play to make sense

Our curious eyes connected again

Connected like a lost kiss
finding the lips it belongs to

We drank from this waterfall of belonging

My satisfaction unleashed its grin like a dog
in the night who smelt a bone

Your cassava teeth bit your lower lip in
anticipation of meeting this canine in a loose
corner to see who will get the first bite

There was stage fright

No words had yet been uttered
but stories and poetry had been written
regarding our encounter

Where will it lead?

I chose not to read these words written by the
winds

The cocoa butter on your arms glistened in the
moon light
I couldn't help but stare blindly at your
sculpted frame
Your bare back sung me a song
that forced my tongue in the directions of your
Kilimanjaro

What is your name?

Before the, "w", left the village of my lips
The elders in my saliva
shifted the ivory tiles on my scrabble rack

They unraveled a less obvious but smoother
question

"It's a beautiful evening wouldn't you say?"

A carefully calculated phrase to see the type
of feline I was dealing with

Like a hunter, I had prepared for this
confrontation
Nights upon nights I had practiced and failed
at my encounters to perfect the craft of
seduction

I was now smoother than silk

My words were creamy like butter made from milk
of dairy cows in the
Great Rift Valley in Kenya

I teased subtly like rain clouds in the
Kalahari Desert darkening for a pour

But I did not pour

I showered you with compliments
and scores of tease to unlock your dimples

I played my confidence like alikoto

Spinning circles around you like a hacker
writing an algorithm to explain confusion

My plan was to break your dark velvet skin like
yooyi

So my milkshake order was intentional

For palm wine won't allow me to blow whip cream
playfully in your direction

"I wanted to add more make-up", I joked

I then leaned over to wipe the cream off your
Shai Hill cheek

I took my time journeying
toward your Table Mountain
Allowing each step, to carefully sink into your
personal space

As I wiped and licked off my attack
from your face,
I sensed that your hills were no more shy

Our pupils attracted once more
I could feel you wanting me to be closer

Next thing I know,
you took my hand and placed it on your waist

Like a tour guide you led me into the thick of
the Atiwa rainforest of the dance floor
Synchronizing yourself to the beat of music
falling like rain on our ears

We flowed like a neat mix of oil and water
gliding over each other
Intoxicating ourselves with the night

Once we had drank our fill,
we settled to catch our breath
Reminiscing the evening

My prey was ready for the kill

"Can I have your number?"

A tissue, pen and shy smile were my bow and
arrow
Worthy weapons to acquire my prize

She penned down her number and name,
beaming with butterflies dancing azonto in her
belly

She felt desired and was eager for another
safari chase

But the sun had begun to rise
So I kissed her hand and promised to call
But once I was out of her sight
I threw the number away

I let my cassava fish back into the ocean
I wanted to feel attractive
And make the attracted feel desired

I had achieved that

That's all I was looking for
A night to show that my hunting skills were
intact

My trophy, was a phone number
A phone number, that I was never going to call

Poet's Notes

Aside the interesting ending, my goal with this
poem was to express love or attraction using
African scenery and Ghanaian jargon.

I realized that when it comes to romance,
Western concepts and locations are often used
in portraying love. It is as if Africa and its
cultures are foreign to the subject. I thus
challenged myself to speak on attraction using
things belonging to the African continent.

My visits to South Africa and Kenya made me
lean towards their landscapes. The other terms
were mainly sights from Ghana and things I
experienced in my childhood growing up in
Kaneshie and Sakumono in Accra. Alikoto and
ampe for instance are childhood games of Ghana.
Yooyi on the other hand, is the local name in
Ghana for black tamarind.

I'VE BEEN ROBBED

I woke up at 4:40 AM and found that I have been
robbed

My recent treasured asset that I gained
unexpectedly the day before has been stolen

I didn't get to enjoy it much

How did the thief get into my house?
Was it through the back or front door?

I believe it was through the window

I slept on the couch whilst watching a movie on
the tele'
In hindsight, I should have just gone to the
bedroom

Should I call the police?
What will they be able to do about this?
I do not believe they are qualified to deal
with my unique case

God being so good, my phone was not stolen
I guess I should be grateful

If you find the thief that stole my sleep this
early morning,
please contact me

For I am not done with it

BLIND FAITH

My faith is blind because I am a mountain
A mountain that can't see the valley
or how badly things are going underneath
All I feel is the breeze
The breeze from this Earth and the next
surround my senses and enable me to feel peace

But I can't see this peace

My mind is pointed towards stubbornness
At my peak, I block off all wisdom and sip from
the tea of my confidence

But where does that leave me?

Am I better off for attaining this great blind
success?

My faith climbed the mountain and became one
with it
I thought my sacrifice on this climb was my
strength
I now see that it was my sight that got lost
along the way

So now I don't believe

Will my belief change if I climb down?
Will my tears appear if I get off my highchair?

I would never know unless I try
I thought I conquered my faith by climbing the
mountain
But in conquering the mountain, my faith became
blind
What must I conquer to enable me to see my
greatness?
How high must I jump off to see God once again?

I guess the answer lies in falling from this
great mountain

So, let's fall
Let's fall down with our eyes open

It may be painful

But not as painful as having faith, that can't
see love

PUPPETS

They came in the night and cut the strings
They cut the wires
They cut the…things that made us connected to
them
They cut the swing
They cut the motions
So now we have the notion that we are still in
control

But we are not

We are taught that we have the power to control
this country
We contribute and have a say on what we do as a
nation
We hold the controls
The sticks with the strings
Tugging and pulling hands and feet
Emotions and necks
Yes, we are the ones controlling these puppets

So why aren't they dancing?
Why aren't they dancing as we say they should?

Look,
I pull on this to cause him to jump
But he ignores my gestures

I fall to the floor in disappointment and see a
possible problem

Tangled strings

Yes, that is the problem

We bumped into each other as a people and have
tied our pioto together
This is what we refer to as united
Our unity is a sorry story

of cotton strings tied in the blood
of future generations

We focus on continuing
the chaotic confusion
instead of undoing the crisis
of crisscross strings

It's a puzzle
But unlike sudoku,
this is a game of the mind

Unfortunately, we are entangled deeply
in an illogical blind dream
The puppets move differently
But not because of our confusion

Their moves are ordered by someone else
Someone who came in the night
and cut the strings
Cut the wires
Cut the rings,
that married and made our puppets loyal to
their masters

They are connected to new masters
More experienced in the art of puppetry

From afar, they hide in the clouds
Creating the illusion that we are still in
control
That the confusion is normal
That suffering is life

They rain lies, kidnap truth
and nurture their own proof
That this, is the best we will ever have

It's a play Shakespeare will be proud of

A tragedy that converts

the puppeteer into a puppet
to fight his own fears

Convincing them to dance
to a different tune
than they are used to

But I am confused

Am I the puppeteer?

Or am I...the puppet?

Poet's Notes

Who is in control? This question is one that doesn't get asked often. In this poem I explore the concept of control and the illusion it sometimes carries. I am reminded of how I let me kids sit on my lap, when I am driving the car into the house. They believe they are the ones doing the driving. Who is driving the vehicle known as you? Who is controlling the traffic lights and the placement of the road signs?

Are you the puppeteer or the puppet?

PRIEST

You are not my priest
You're merely a human placed in close proximity
Placed by the cosmos
for reasons unknown to me
Like the placement of stars in the universe

I don't know why you ask me questions
I know I started the conversation
but I don't like how it's going
Can we skip to the end?
Why are we passing here?
This is the wrong way!
Yet, I don't know where I am going

So why am I mad at you?

You who have been warm with me
this cold night
You who gave me a blanket of kindness
when I spewed insults your way

Strangers aren't meant to be
this optimistic
Maybe you are my lucky star
So I guess it's okay
to show you my dark side
Maybe you can save me from these
Star Wars within

You are not my priest
And this bar is not a church
But I am a long way from salvation
So I guess, you will have to do

IF I COULD DANCE

If I could dance

I would move uncontrollably
to the snares and cymbals
I would allow the strings of the piano
to play on my tendons and move my legs
magically across the dance floor
to thump out the bass in a battle

I would twerk my joints as I slide to the left
and then right indecisively
Reacting to the shockwaves of electronic organ
melodies playing traffic conductor to my
movements

My hips would be possessed
Confessing its sins in cosine functions
I co-sign something
when the beat is aggressive and fast
It allows me to take a pause, and then laugh
As I explode into a fit of tai chi battle poses
with a face
Teleporting through emotions

My hands will communicate #
in a new sign language
Yes, I design language
The type that causes your eyes to pop out and
stay glued to my expressions
The type that causes you to rewind
and share to a friend
The type you want to speak about but fear you
can't because your feet divorced you
Divorced you a long time ago because you
couldn't let go of your feelings

So let go

Let your heart be alive

with the sound of music
Let rhythm caress you into a groove

Feel the highlife
Feel the house
Feel the bounce
Feel the unexplainable anointing
tickling your confidence to bust a move
You can start with a nod and express for
satisfaction, your joy in a spin
A jerk
A flick
You can learn a trick,
to blow our minds
To show that our science of movement
is one of cause and effect

But I am afraid to dance

I am afraid to profess my love to the floor
I cuff my feet to my thoughts
Forbidding them from going out to explore
where the music will take them
I forbid my heart from drumming the same beat
Because I am afraid

I am afraid someone will see me dancing

And laugh

Poet's Notes

I used to love dancing when I was younger. The
highlight for me at a kid's party was the dance
competition. My special move was the running
man.

In high school, I loved it whenever there was a
jam (a school disco night). I had a dancing
partner (who is now a DJ. Not surprised at all)
who was 1 year my senior. Strangely enough we
would only talk when there was a jam. There was
no agreement between us but...we just knew that
we were going to open the dance floor and close
it. We both knew what we were in for and danced
our troubles away when the opportunity came.

These days I am a bit shy about dancing. Maybe
it's because I can't do the running man to the
songs.

DADA B BOYFRIEND

My dada b boyfriend bought me a dada b teddy
bear so that I can have some dada b dreams

He said I should get used to living like a queen
and dream like my life was on the big screen

Not the 15-inch TV that is in mummy's room
but the 50-inch LED that has HD and 3D

My dada b boyfriend says we should improve our
communication

He says I have to get rid of my Nokia 3210
forget about text and move on to social media
where we can DM

I have always wanted an iPhone I hear its jer!

My brother says the latest one in China can
hold 4 sims

This is good, for now I can have Glo, Airtel
Tigo, Vodafone and MTN

When I told my dada b boyfriend about the
device, he said having that phone is a sin

Immediately he travelled abroad and bought me
the latest iPhone, Apple Watch and added an
iPad, just for flex

One morning I went over to my dada b boyfriends
house to check out its contents and specs
There was this black box called DSTV which had
over 100 channels, even one for pets
There was also this app on the TV called
Netflix that I hear is a magic stream of movies
and series where one can go and fetch

He says that this DSTV and Netflix is something
that dada b's in Ghana can't live without
And that I should get used to it if I want to be
his spouse

My dada b boyfriend has a dada b name,
Sean Kofi

He is 6ft tall, weighs 76 kg and has a sexy six
pack

Sean aka SK, has dada b skin,
with a sweet accent that can make a girl like me
sin

Americanized and brofolized making him sound
like a CEO of an enterprise

My dada b boyfriend believes that he is royalty

"I am dada b with hard labour",
he says convincingly

Which simply means he does house chores some

House chores being...
hovering the carpets, putting clothes in a
washing machine,
and occasionally washing the car when he is
going to use it

My dada b boyfriend even has a dada b computer
He doesn't use a PC or a laptop
He says his computer is named after one of
Jesus's disciples, Mark
So he has this fresh computer with the bitten
apple from the Garden of Eden on it that never
rots

As for my dada b boyfriend dierrrrrrr his
gadgets are too posh

He too he dey rosh
He sprays perfume on himself every morning
As if he dey kill mosquito
He also buys sunglasses, shoes and new shadda
every two weeks

He even uses dada b condoms
Durex!
He says he doesn't do Fiesta condoms
I however told him that I'm a Christian
So dada b condom or not, no sex

He says I dey flex
So I took him to church
For the occasion, he bought a new cover for his
iPad pro and used it as his Bible
The cover matched his shadda roff!

Can you imagine?

This darling of mine dierrrrrrr he be too
much!

Anyways he has travelled, so I am using his
house as my house for now

I have to go and watch the Kardashians on DSTV
to keep up with him

Catch you on the gram!

HOPELESS LOVE

Allow my thoughts to breathe
the same air as you
For my journey to your heart is long
Without a compass, direction or bearing,
I walk
For each step I know not whether I move closer
or further from your heart
Truly I'm blind
I curse my eyes not though
For through my eyes, I see your beauty
Sometimes I wish you weren't so beautiful
Seas of lessons have flooded my shores
Nine seas I have encountered, each singing the
same song
"Forget her heart"

I cannot

Why I journey though, I know not
Reasons as many as the seconds of my past,
alone or together,
never justify to my mind or others,
why I journey to your soul

Your soul completes me
Defeats me
Gives me enough strength to rise and start over
again
Start over in search of feelings

Your feelings

Towards my hearts cry to you

HEADACHE

There is a sound that betrays pain
An invisible thumping that translates this
internal sound into,

ADJEI!

A vibrant rhythm announcing itself
as a,

head...ache

A head...ache

Perforating my mind and causing an earth...quake
Nerves...wait
For a response from the cerebrum
I need a time machine to rewrite this
curriculum

Black pen, blue pen, it doesn't matter
I don't have the answer to this question that
devours my brain
My headache is not of pain but of questions
Oppression of this black mind is just an
artist's impression

I'm 30 minutes stressing
I've only got my name on the paper
I'm not even past the first question
My headache is getting stronger
I guess it is because the thought of cheating
has crossed my mind and is creating a new world
order
I'm really at the border
The option is looking viable
If I don't do it, I will probably get a disorder
I guess I need some water
I welcome water in the form of sweat on my palms
and tell it to raise the alarm

The calculator is of no help
Time is ticking like a bomb
So I pause and fidget
Calculate the physics of my life
I think I have failed this paper twice
The answer I have put down is not right
At least I am making progress
I'm now answering the second question thrice
Why did they change the paper at the last
minute from multiple choice?
My headache is now getting a louder voice
Anyway, I try to remember the formula
A over D plus E
But what is A, D or E?
I try to put my mind at ease
but question 5,6,7 and 8 all depend on E

I wake up and realize I'm free
I have three days to write the paper,
practice, redeem myself and know the answer to E
Pass the paper, hope the calculator helps me to
breathe
To get confusion out of my head
And end its shopping, spree

Poet's Notes

This poem is me without the dream bit. I was in high school writing my Add Math final exam. I was looking at my mates asking for extra paper and followed suite to look like I knew what I was doing - I did not know what I was doing.

UNITY

Brotherhood, Ubuntu, Family?
Family however fights family
People of the same country fight one another
Mother sells daughter to father because he
cannot get enough?
That's our unity?

Unity is in the bed having sex!
That's why we do not see her

Unity is in her puberty
After she falls pregnant and endures her
suffering,
maybe, just maybe, she will wake up to her true
purpose

Brotherhood, Ubuntu, Family?
Family wasn't always like this
Unity was a beautiful girl
Her complexion was like that of a mud hut in the
shade and beach sand in the light
Her smile carried peace

What caused it then?

Dare you not say white man
White man just put gloves on the hands ready to
swing the axe
This was just to ensure efficiency
The truth is that we are the ones to blame
We introduced Unity to Greed
Ever since then, it's not been the same

From drugs to alcohol, sex and money
Greed showed Unity another side of life
She was blinded
The little cute girl that once brought our
hearts together, now has a boyfriend

Brotherhood, Ubuntu, Family?
How did we let this happen?

Don't you know?
Can't you see?
We are being deceived
Our eyes are blinded by Greed
Therefore, we accept him
See him as a prince
Yet, he is a curse
The curse of Africa
The one who has made us lose Unity

Unity is so long gone it makes me sick when I
hear people talk about her
When the family of Greed came for her hand in
marriage, all we got were fifteen cows
We rejoiced gladly for the wealth we had
received
We all got what we wanted
Greed after all was very wealthy
He ensured we all got what our greedy hearts
desired

After the wedding she left
Discarded from our family
No longer a part of us

I wish I could see the day when brotherhood
will mean more
When cultures will fight no more
Tribes kill no more
When country and country in the continent of
Africa will see themselves as equal
I must be smoking good weed
For that my friend, is what books and our dreams
will talk about,
but our eyes, shall never see

Brotherhood, Ubuntu, Family

BLACK PEARLY GATES

The black pearly gates open to us an
opportunity of a lifetime
Streets of gold and mansions upon mansions
decorate the sidewalks of this magnificence
I hear we walk on clouds here
The fashion trend is white only
Yet, I see many black and brown folk scattered
all over
This is a different boat we're sailing on
The sea is not made of time
The winds here are filled with song and carry
no coffins or sickness
The lion and gazelle are friends in this ark
Today they laugh at their morbid history and
smile their way into the future
The slut and her lover take a walk in a garden
of dandelions, scorpions, snakes and roses
The pastor who condemned them is nowhere to be
found
So are some of the choir
There are few armed robbers, addicts and drunks
here
The so-called lesbians, gay and transgender
In fact, the whole LGBTQ community has
representation here
Everyone is getting along
Even the police and the community
The good guys too are here
Some Muslims, Buddhists, voodoo practitioners,
juju men and even atheists
Were they pretending?
Or was I judging not knowing their inner being
Just because the gates were rumored to be
pearly,
doesn't mean they can't be…
black

AMOS

My name is Amos Quito
A mosquito drinking blood like pito
I'm a Luis Figo
Skillful
I love to go down to the thigh of the chick with
a kilo of booty

Amos has a thing for big things to him they are
a beauty

The mosquito today is a ninja
A threat that mankind remembers
West African Mafia killing all its contenders
The God Father
Second only to AIDS and maize
Think about it for a second,
this assassin deserves praise
Suburbs know its name
Mansions to the same
Even air-conditioners can't keep them out its
insane

They use Raid as their perfume
Smoke mosquito coils and get high past their
curfew
Their favorite movie is Twilight
I think they're sponsored by Red Bull
Which they drink a lot
So they're silent and careful with their
camouflage
Their favorite rap group must be Terror Squad
They also like listening to Wiz Kid and Niki
Minaj on Channel 0
They love black people unopposed
They are processing visas to get to the US
through the post into the white house
The UN has been fighting for them to be wiped
out

I really hate it when they come through when
it's lights out

One mosquito,
but you'll think its ten mosquitoes
Giving you tattoos like Miami Ink
They never give you rest
They think they are the coolest insects yet
They were Ray Bans with night vision just to
look their best
So when we try to get them,
it seems like we're out fishing
They stand back with a pose and laugh at us
dissing
"Clap louder humans, try and catch us we are not
pigeons!"

Clap!

Finally, I got one
But my celebration is short lived
To kill this silly insect, I had to slap the
thigh of my chick
She's pissed
Mosquitos are still laughing at me
They are slick
Will kill one of their own for a silly joke?
They are sick insects!

Is this the result of incest?
Killing people like banks interest?
Amos is in my palm sending a prayer out,
destressed
Thinking of the wine he sucked at the various
clubs
He met Sylvia,
who hit the jackpot and screamed,
"I'll kill ya!"
Hopped on to kiss the hand of pretty Matilda
Didn't have enough so went onto build a,
malaria mansion,

Amos was the builder on Tiffany
Sucked like vampires in Twilight and had an
epiphany
That he will die on my hands as I enhanced the
tip of the,
kinetic force
Which will force malaria to the wall
But Amos was only a messenger
Malaria was the boss

My name is Amos Quito
A mosquito drinking blood like pito
I'm skillful like Figo
I have a boss that kills all people
Almost killed a million in 2008, too slow
11,000 Ghanaians, some infected on Ring Road
Fear my pace
I'm a ghost without a face
So you killed Amos
But I always win the race

I'm Malaria!

This message was brought to you by kind
courtesy of the association of mosquitoes at
the Korle lagoon

Poet's Notes

*The idea for this piece came about when a
friend personified a mosquito biting incident
by calling the mosquito, Amos. I asked for the
reason and found that the phrase, "A mosquito"
can be rearranged to make the name "Amos Quito".
From this naming ceremony, I decided to create a
humorous piece based on this character.*

PICTURE WHAT A PICTURE PICTURES

It's funny what a picture captures
within a chapter
With a press of a button
a device begins to answer
Turns light into a dancer
Swallows time and moments like a pill
In a still
Holds color within a capture
Hostage with emotions
A summary of the commotion of the past
held in storage to make a pass,
a story, an album, a catalog, make a glass,
of possibilities accessible
Let's drink and take the past along with us
Reversing time now belongs to us
We rewind better than VCRs and an om-ni-bus
Its priceless
So picture what a picture pictures
Real time is not right but the picture will
still whisper the before
Kidnap the now and the more
You can now see what happened in 94
So even though you didn't exist you can miss
Reminisce, the feeling of before in a kiss
Of a picture and your mind
Timestamps they are these pictures,
they enable remember to rewind
Capture the details, the retail - value of the
picture is priceless, and travels further than
email to your heart
What's a megabyte to a heart?
The visual is critical to make us fall apart
and come together
Our smartphones now tell the weather
The little circles at the back steal time and
get the better,
side of the frame
They say God created the stage
He may not have made the camera,

but wanted us to save
Moments like plants,
to help us see the plans of destiny manifest
into purpose like fans
The Chinese type that folds out
So that we can roll out
Memories like film from back in the day to
throw out sadness
A picture is a glass of gladness
Enabled by God to show us his kindness
To remind us of his most precious creation
The wonderful energy called…

Life

WHAT PILLOW ARE YOU SLEEPING ON?

You slept on a pillow of broken promises
Like a cracked pot you were scattered whilst
the cracker milked the jack pot
The broken pot was a blot in our history
A plot to rewrite our story
dissolving the truth
So that our children will be confused about
their heritage

But they were not

You see, some of us sleep on pillows of hope
So broken promises don't have the power to choke
us in our dreams
We are the seam
Joining our hopes and dreams together
With our people rewriting the catastrophe known
as colonization

Many of our dreamers got lost in the stream
Some we remember and for others it seems their
dreams together became the foundation of what
we know as Africa

Mothers and wives were abandoned for this dream
Fathers and warriors were lost in the stream of
blood
Blood that gushed forth and broke down the
gates to freedom

But freedom isn't enough

The freedom we were given is a pillow of lies
Lies that pretends to comfort and ease the
burdens on our heads and lives
A pillow of nails goring our skulls
Robbing us of our intellect and identity
So we don't know who we are

We have come so far on this journey and just
realized
that the forward we seek - is an illusion

We have come so far in our pain
that we have forgotten that our roots hold the
answers we seek

We are asleep on a pillow of freedom
given to us by our colonizers
A pillow that locks us into a nightmare we are
unable to escape
The pillow is a shackle forcing us to sleep
Stopping us from waking up and living in truth

We sleep in suffering and pain so horrific
that we have made it the new normal
A walking dead reality show broadcasted
for the world to view for free

But there is a truth that changes this story

The truth is a dreadlocked African with a beard
and animal skin roaring from within

But we are afraid

Afraid that this lion within will devour us as
we explore our inner strength
We are afraid that this revolution will leave a
stench

How bad can the stench be?
Is it as bad as the broken promises
you slept on?
Is it as bad as the raping of our mothers,
sisters and African resources?

There is a fire within us boiling water
underneath our brown skins
But I see no bubbles and steam

I see no eruption, no volcano
All I see are hills and mountains that whisper
and lament
As if the troubles we swallow don't affect us
As if the troubles we swallow don't give us
mental diarrhea
As if the troubles we swallow, don't push us to
deal with the issue

What slow poison have we swallowed?
What bed have we laid and are sleeping on?

I don't know

What I know is that some of us never slept on a
bed
The pillow we had was grass
So when the ant or mosquito bites
We wake up

We wake up

And make our dreams, come true

BLIND DREAMING

I allow raindrops to fall on my eyes
To bring a surprise of blindness
To bring a design
Reinforce the distance,
to bring a demise of illusions
True perception is the solution in this
revolution
The raindrops is my ablution
The deception of this real world, is a matrix
polluted

I therefore decide to be blind for a time
In a distance of 5 years in a system sublime
I try to run in my mind, a television
A television of definitions to help complete
the mission

So the raindrops fall on my eyes, I arise
In calculating the vision,
questions arrive
Questions survive past the blindness
Questions baptize
Brutality to get reality
Questions capsize
Assumptions to find serenity
But the truth is deprived

I thus bleach myself to find the remedy
I bleach myself white to fine dine and wine the
enemy
For homo sapiens no longer create rainbows
They spray mold, all over their rivers as they
corrupt and crave gold

I stay cold, though the sun is out
I stay old, drinking in the wisdom of the dead
with clout
I stay bold…like a font
This dream isn't what I want

So I allow the storm to fall and blanket me from
the top,
in blindness
Not to continue living in shyness
but to resurrect...in another dream

PRINCESS

The term princess is not reserved for the
daughters of royalty
It's an honor passed down to a daughter by one
who takes care of their own
So when I call you a princess,
understand that I speak more about what is
vital
Not wealth and a title
I speak about character and cycles,
of the beauty within your soul

I want to be myself around you
Myself however, is not prince enough for you
Princes rode to your castle and returned to
their kingdoms without conquer
I wonder, if I want to be a prince

If a prince means
serving you, making you smile and being your
friend
Then Princess, tell me you love me

A friend I try to be
A lover I want to be
Silence defines your beauty better than any
element under the sun
Aligned with the stars, you become a zodiac
May our children be born under your star

You don't believe in fairy tales
But you are in one
Just because your eyes do not show it,
does not mean it does not exist
A whole Earth exists in your palm
Seas, mountains, clouds from afar
The lines on your palms are rainbows
Each finger represents an angel
Black coffee with milk and honey legs

The valley led by treasures reveal your nails
as rubies,
feet as diamonds and legs as a scepter to hold
it upon

Many ways there are to describe your beauty
Should we begin the never-ending description,
of a princess?

DZIFA

Allow my mind to wonder,
on your heart from afar
Tattoo my devotion, to your lungs like a scar
Make me feel acceptance,
hold my hand, you're a star
Cocoa I send to your chocolate senses in a car,
to invoke dreams
I send you on fantasy travels in Accra
I marvel at your grace, at your waist, at your
bar,
of curves that I know, are massaged at a spa
Join me as we flee, from Accra to Dakar
Every day you are new, you're a tune, a guitar
You burn up my passion, like a Cuban cigar
Your eyes interpret the meaning, it opens a jar
Freeing up your smile, to play my guitar
It's bizarre
The wave of your hand is by far
Exquisite like a fan, in the hands of a Czar
You create magic in my drink, you're a bar
Your laughter is a seed that I hear from afar
It grows in my heart, like the trees in Qatar
Your curves are endless, like the songs of
guitar
Please don't leave me, don't say au revoir
From my words it is clear, that my heart is ajar
I will write about you, till it's heard in the
stars
Of the beautiful girl, that I met at a bar
Who stirred my emotions, like a baker to flour
To take a slice of love,
one evening in Accra

TIME, CONVERSATION & FEAR

Time

Time is a musician
A master playing the harp, flute and the lyre
When I see you, it plays the African drum
When you smile, it sings with the voice of the
waterfalls
When we smile and our heart beats as one
It stops

Though a master musician, it draws it skill from
love
When it stops, it listens to the music we make
It halts the air around, allows us to exist and
breathes in our happiness
In trying to understand,
it is angered and quickens its pace
In being stubborn, it plays on the atɛntɛben,
a lullaby to send our eyes away
But your feet
Beautiful and quick
Brown and fine in texture, like the bass
Dances to whatever song is played
and fuels my passion

Conversation

Words sewed together into sentences
and exchanged with emotion
Your words and mine seem to know each other
when we speak
Without even our lips moving,
they escape and whisper to us our true thoughts
By just looking at you,
I feel your words searching me
Searching for my words and where they are
hiding

We are tailors of love my dear

We sew with silk threads, compassion and
happiness
In our absence, our work goes on

Fear

I fear that if I don't tell you how I feel,
my soul will refuse to exist
I am afraid of where we are going
But more scared of not being with you
I fear the day you tell me you love me,
my heart will beat out of my chest
I fear the day I touch you passionately
For I will not want to ruin your beauty

The day I fear most however,
is not the day that I die
But the day I hurt you without a reason

That, will make me cry

YOUR DREAMING

If poetry was lost, we would not exist
Chapters written exist to breathe life to the
never-ending fairy tale
Your perfume awakened my love
In your absence, my longing wrote this poem

Take me into your world to enable understanding
Free yourself from the world to enable our love
to grow

Its midnight; your door is ajar
But my footsteps you will hear not
Today I leave my door ajar
Waiting on your footsteps
Nourish your soul with the happiness my love
feeds
Forever I am yours to recollect

The fuel to keep the fire burning lies within
us
The wood from my forest alone can do so much
The same story is told about your woods
Children gather from yours and mine to relight
the fire for a story

What says your heart?
Tell me about your feelings
The desires that your lips and heart only know
of
Feed my soul,
for I am hungry and can only eat your love

Love is immortal, it can never die
Resurrection is possible when there is a will
If the will is strong enough, we can resurrect
Not in this world, but in your dream

THE PERFECT SENTENCE

I feel it coming
A wonderful, bubbly spirit
Capturing my senses
Taking me to your soul

The roses on your chest blossom with colour
The fragrance arising,
tempts me to touch your significance

In a space of the air that surrounds you
Laughter is born

Your smile brings out the sun
That's why your feeling is warm
Though you do not write poetry
You are a poem on your own

The words and phrases,
conjunctions that join to form you,
the perfect sentence
Can only be found in the dictionaries,
of the future - and the past

WIND QUESTIONS

And the wind asked,
"Do you know what love is?"

I thought I did
Then I knew I didn't
Then I knew what it was
But did not experience it till she walked into
my life

Beauty never asked me so gently to fall in love

And the wind asked,
"Describe her"

She is diamonds sister and pearl's cousin
Her smile gives summer strength to make flowers
blossom
Soft as a baby, her touch is gentle
God blessed me with his daughter for a lover

And the wind asked
"Where should I carry you?"

Far across the ocean to her voice,
her poise, to her hands to rejoice
For love kissed me in the face
My heart is my voice

"Where did you find her?",
the wind asked

I didn't find her
Love did
She was lost as I was
Looking for a horse to ride through a valley,
to a land she could cross,
over the border to a land,
where peace was not cross

I met her hand,
you blew her perfume grand
I gazed into her eyes
She smiled in mine

After an hour
We are in each other's arms

To find love,
one can't be prepared
However, one bearing patience,
will receive a prize, well deserved

LOVE IS PAIN

I can't deal with this monster taking over
inside
I tried, I tried,
tears flow and sweat pain

If only she knew,
If only she could see my complexity
Understand that I have been there before
Knocked on the door repeatedly
Got an answer as if there was no one indoors

If only she understood,
that I live like it's my last
Not regretting things in the past
If only she understood

But how can she understand?
How can she understand
when you lie about love and apologize for it?
Talk about it and act differently?

If only you knew I told her about you

But you wished you never knew

How you cried and wished it weren't true
Now I wish I was consumed with other matters
But I can't ignore this other matter that angers
your heart

I know it hurts
But pain tells us where we are on the map of
love
It feels like you are dying,
I know that you are fighting to stay sane
But love is a pill that is pain and beauty
For now, it's just pain
Pain because I told you the truth
Not because you will forgive me

But because, I will never forgive myself if you
got hurt

But here I am hurting you
Stabbing you with the truth
For something so worthless

For something worthless - and greedy

As selfishness

13 WAYS OF LOOKING AT A BUTT

I love ass…
Sorry, I just got distracted by,
duna, isinqa, etu, egbi, culo, matako and bunda
What I meant to say is,
I love ass…king

Buttocks abbreviated as "butt"
is both an excuse and asset
with pun intended

It makes the excuse of ending
in a single or double TT,
depending on how strong
you want your tea,
when admiring or making an excuse

This tangible asset is available in all shapes,
sizes and attitudes
Because we love them,
I will say it has a latitude and longitude,
due to how easy it is to locate them,
how long we stare at them
and the duration we carry an excuse

It's quite the pregnant case we ass…imilate for
ourselves
A backside story with a surprise each time we
read
Without BUTTs
G-strings would not have puffed to popularity

Butts are not gender specific
They as…sociate with all as…semblies and
individuals
Their impact to society is ass-trological in
the positive and negative
An ass-sessment of the negatives reveal a smell
and drug as the main as…sasins on as…singment
to give BUTTs a baaaaad name

You see a smell comes from BUTTs

Whether Beyonce, Gaga, Moesha or Puffs
Never too pleasant especially
when tenant to eggs,
and dairy products eating through like hungry
birds

Now let's talk about cigarette BUTTs
The coldest assassin
The ones that last longer than the smokers who
puff
Their owners are always in a gamble to bluff,
their lungs away which scream whilst coughing,
enough

These BUTTs kill more than the drugs in a bay
Heroine, marijuana, tikk and cocaine
What a killer
What a killer
Tobacco is insane
Yet a legal weapon and excuse for not staying
humane

The cigarette BUTT is classy
You smoke, puff, pull and give a long smoke
winding
No adverts needed and it still sells more than
icing
The scary packages indeed don't affect the
pricing

As mentioned earlier, BUT is also used for
excuses

BUT I wasn't home
It wasn't shown
BUT I didn't hear or
wasn't near my phone

The excuses are numerous
and vary in truth
A fart is not needed
to stink as proof

This very poem
is nothing but an excuse,
to BUTT into an interesting conversation with
you

BLACK MAN

A black man's road is never paved
In the beginning, this mahogany is filled with
rage
His dark soiled mind is filled with pain
everyday
Cultivating a world, he can never change
When this diamond was seen, he was called a
slave
Slaved in chains all his day
The charcoal was tossed in the fire, he was put
in the cage
Even the Doberman laughed, when he heard his
name

Now I try to understand, comprehend, ponder,
wonder why, skin color in their eyes has to be
only white?
Is it right that the white man dominates the
night by running free whilst the black man is
hiding in the tree?

Why do we constantly bring each other down in
hate!
Instead of moving forward,
our shadows have mastered the art of moon
walking
Thus, the whole Africa looks like a mental
institution
Yet, it was the very same place the first
university was born
The blackboards of our education told some
white lies
White lies that erased black time and made us
blind
But for how long?
How long are we going to be blind my brothers?
For our ancestors and forefathers are
constantly crying

That's why the grass is always wet in the
morning
Dumb creatures
Even the blind man is better off
For the blind man sees only black and
nothingness
Whilst a black man sees no opportunity when
swimming in gold

Yes, we were sold!
We were slaves, we were told
Black fought for our freedom
We are free, we are bold
But they tore up our identity
Made us flee, we were broke
They pissed on our freedom
Took our dreams and our hope

But I refuse
I refuse to leave my road unpaved
Refuse to be called a slave
Resort to corruption
Allow greed to run in my veins
Dismantle my ways
Worsen the pain
Just like a cane
Hitting my mane
Going whack, whack into the stain,
of blood crying, roaring, devouring mourning,
every black night and morning
for peace to dominate, relegate, eliminate, pain
into a lake
From the black onyx lake in my mother's womb I
came
With brain power moving
11 by 11
24/7
Faster than those who died in the 9/11 getting
into heaven
I am definitely in God's plan
I am a question in the white society,

because I am not like them
So, let me ask you a question

Why did white man change brown sugar from cane
sugar to white sugar?
Is it because the brown reminded them of the
blacks?
But white sugar in black tea?
Couldn't they not see
That their efforts will not breed,
white tea, so why,
steal brown from brown sugar?
Like Michael Jackson did in the night
by changing from black to white
Later on singing the song,
It does not matter if you are black or white

Black may never be accepted
Even by their own
It's literally a black beat box
Beating on its own

I have refused to be this black man that denies
the acceptance
I refuse to be this brother
that cries about repentance
So though I've found myself
I realize others are still blind
And that I walk a lonely road
with brothers and sisters,
who have shackles,

on their minds

Poet's Notes

This poem is the first spoken word piece I ever wrote. I wrote this in 2005 at the University of Zululand in South Africa. I performed the poem alongside some other wonderful poets. I wonder if they ever continued in their poetic expression. The poem has been edited from its original form, but the concept and message remain the same.

AKOLA BONI

Naughty boy needs music to get high!
But life is a lie
and I lie in a bed of spikes
live life in the mental light
I fly

With wings to take me further than a seagull,
I've got eyes like an eagle
Trust, my sight is pretty lethal

Penetrate my vision and you will see,
death, massacre, silly things like, HIV

I am an African
But I don't feel proud to be one
Roll up in my streets, you will feel foul to be
one

Our pain is messed up
Light the fire back again
I will call up the shadows,
tutor you all back to black again

I again, lost regulation of my breath,
'cos meditation took me to a higher level
I am calibrating my sixth sense
Pour incense, all over my head
Curse my tongue to speak wisdom all over again

And I will die
Why?
'Cos I oblige, cry,
tears of black water like Jesus did when he
died
I try to, menstruate the blood of my people
producing garbage
It hurts like hell, but I volunteer up for the
damage
'cos I feel the beat

Beat to kill eat
Out of my system, so hunger comes into existence

I hunger for the love of my black child, black
brother, black mother
Lord give me lyrics so that we can just feel
each other
The tiger in me is under arrest
'cos there is so much stress,
the giant in me gave up to the test

But I'll leave you with a quote by BIG
to let you know that your hopes ain't behind me
I'll fight to the finish

"The weak or the strong, who got it going on?"

Why the hell do you think they call me naughty
boy in this song?

Poet's Notes

This is one of those poems that can be
performed as poetry, spoken word or rap. The rap
version can be found on my debut album WTF? On
streaming platforms. The quote "the weak or the
strong, who got it going on?" is from the track
"Dead Wrong" of the Born Again album by The
Notorious B.I.G.

Around 1999 and early 2000 when the album came
out, I was beginning to get into hip-hop. This is
one of the albums I listened to heavily at the
time.

THE BULLET

You don't need a gun to shoot a bullet
Chemistry to create poison
All you got to do is make choices

Yours shoots a bullet that cheats death
Instead of killing me,
it makes me feel less...appreciated
Depreciated I feel,
my will falls down like the rain
The train forgot it needs the railway track to
sway
To move, to push
I was pushed by you,
and forgotten like the train,
so I cannot...move

That's your bullet

I sit here, trying to pull it

Out of this train of a body that got
sidetracked
Sidetracked with rejection as a passenger to
hijack,
my heart

Though I apologize by heart
Your heart has stopped beating
I am traumatized in part

I no longer recognize this flower that stands
before me
My questions and explanations ricochet on her
dead petals to bore me
The moment she pulled the trigger,
sadness devoured me

She killed herself

She killed herself with a smile and a glass of
wine

I died slowly
Drowning in shock and vines,
of heart ache crying internally
I am stuck in time
Hanging on to hope on a cliff that rhymes,
With death and confusion
Their rap is sublime
For though I am dying,
every breath I take is my inner me trying
Trying to fight to reestablish a connection
A connection that can save this relationship
from death

But bullets don't return phone calls
And my Fante butterfly on this gray morning,
doesn't want to pick up - her phone

Poet's Notes

*Have you ever hurt someone unknowingly and been
unable to contact them to find out what you did
because they don't want to talk to you? That
situation is the inspiration for this piece.*

*In a time of no smartphones, Whatsapp or
Telegram. I was blocked of by my girlfriend at
the time. Someone who I had spoken to an hour
ago and been cool with was now hostile and
uninterested in seeing me or hearing my voice.*

*I went crazy that afternoon and that pain in
heart feels like a bullet killing you slowly.
Love is indeed dangerous.*

MOS DEF

I wasn't perfect
Dropped out of high school with a purpose
Perfect score of kissing all the girls in
detention
My dick was at attention, when history was
present
Because the teacher was boring, and I was making
out with...
Sorry, I can't remember the name
But her hand job was insane
Had to be careful not to make sounds when I came
Failed tests a dozen times like I was deaf
It's ironic how I wanted to be a rapper like Mos
Def
Yet I went to private school
My whole life was cool
I had a face to match to make the honey's drool
Yet I dropped out of high school, with an
attitude
Started taking drugs, selling coke, breaking
mama's rules
Saw the world
Travelled to America as a mule
Got confused with whether drugs or I was being
used
But the cash was worth it
Was glued to money like a pervert
My clients were rich
I had the swag to sell it
Mad credit
Used prostitutes like debit cards
Cars were nothing but an item to be flossed

I did all this at 16
My quick scheme to get rich seemed a little
like something you all see on the big screen
I thought about this when I pulled down this
girl's jeans

Made love to her like Antonio Banderas in that
Desperado scene
Then I black out

I wake up bleeding with screaming thoughts in
my head
Weakened to allow the thoughts to be audible
Instead, I make an attempt to be decent
Limp all the way with reason
To end my life with another's semen seems like a
road filled with demons,
three strangers,
dangers, mixed with blood stuck in my ass hole
Hoping by this time my mother will be at home

I opened the door
Didn't bother to ring the bell at all
Heard my mother throwing insults at me through
the wall
I ignored
Proceeded to my room where I locked
Stopped in the bathroom to take a look at my
watch

5 AM

I've been knocked out for 5 hours
Life is good until three guys jump you like
cowards
Why?
Because my life is good and theirs sour
Dudes I rubbed the wrong way by spitting on
their power
In a club on a Sunday
I was pissed off and in someway
Caused a scene, threw money
Took two of their girls on my campaign

It felt good

Taking doesn't reveal its books

Like chess, I guess my actions teamed up with my
enemies' rook
Got to me and took,
my pants down
Hands down this situation was a mad town
One by one they pulled their dicks,
raped me till I passed out for 5 hours

Now I'm no longer a pretty boy
Just a fucked-up boy in the shower
In the next three hours, I'll be dead

Found in the shower,
with blood covering my entire,
lower body
I never meant harm to nobody
So how come I was raped by three guys before 40?

I guess you could blame it on my desire for
power

It's funny
With all this money I never got to be a rapper

So this here is my first mixtape
Send it to Mos Def
Tell him this legends life,

was a mistake

Poet's Notes

This poem is inspired by the 2003 movie, "I'll Sleep When I'm Dead". I write the poem as the character Davey, played by Jonathan Rhys Meyers. You could say this poem serves as some hidden context to the characters short life. I advise you watch the movie to better appreciate the poem.

FLY

They say one plus one can be equal to three if
you try hard enough

Logic never made miracles,
or made it comprehensible
The supernatural never looks sensible
Yet, always seems to be happening right before
our eyes
Begging for us to believe

All I wanted to do was fly
I never understood why the birds of the air had
that option
Why we masters had to float on metal to surf the
winds
It's part of the reason why I had a hard time
believing in Jesus as the Messiah
Surely the son of God could have displayed his
magnificence by soaring through the air in a
single bound
Two Jews however visualized that supernatural
feat
Giving rise to Superman

There is something about floating in the air at
ones will
I have experienced it numerous times in my
dreams but never in reality
Nothing in the Bible explains how to do this

I have looked beyond religion
Into the dark books to find ways to fly
All have failed or scared me enough to
understand why Jesus never flew when on Earth

I was obsessed with the idea
Eventually, I realized the only way to do this
was to have faith

After a climb to the apex of Mount Afadjato,
I leapt into the air
With my faith in hand,
I began to fly

I flew all over the world
Over sea and islands
Across plains and farms

I flew with the horses of Wales as they
competed
And with the children of Ethiopia as they ran

In the end,
I landed on the clouds and decided to stay
Never wishing to touch the ground again

SHOULD I GIVE A CEDI TO THE KID ON THE STREET

Should I give a cedi to the kid on the street?
Should I give a cedi to the kid on the street?

This question runs through my mind as I find
myself, caught-in-traffic
Boy looks at me with a look saying,
"I, don't, have it"
Grabs my window with eyes looking like a drug
addict,
and says,
"Nsuo k3k3"
Only water

How bad is his smell?
Are his clothes dirty enough?
Is his hair sandy and rough?
Is he hungry?
Is he skinny and not buff?

I try to answer these questions before the
light turns green
An interview he does not have time for
He is trying to survive before he hits thirteen
13 O'clock - its Lunchtime Rhythms on Joy 99.7 FM
I'm wondering whether by not giving this guy
money, whether I am not sinning

My head is spinning
Is his sadness genuine?
His t-shirt is actually feminine
Miley Cyrus
His fashion statement shows his hustle is ahead
of him

Should I give a cedi to the kid on the street?
On my right is this middle-aged guy, about 35,
passing by
He asks for a few coins just to get by
He is not disabled

I guess the coins enable him to be on the street
longer
So he makes more than even the street hawker
He is not looking for water
His dream drink to your surprise,
is probably Johnny Walker
So, he is a stalker; this kid is in search for
some order
Yet my decision is not made
For there is another kid in the corner
Refugee, cutie
Wearing a Barcelona Jersey, Messi
Searching the trash for breakfast

Who should I give a cedi to?
Country man, or Messi?
For we are all brothers
Coming from one father and mother
But Messi is light skinned

Should I discriminate now?

Before I answer that question,
I dribble Messi a few rounds
Where is your mother, father?
Where are you from?
Birthday?
There is no time for these questions
It will be green in the next 30 seconds

The money in my hand was for a Coca Cola
What do I lose by giving country man the cedi?
What will he buy with it?
Does he get a discount when he goes to visit,
the plantain seller on the other side of the
street?
I try to preach
But does he even understand the English that I
speak?
Who is God to him?
Plus am I one of God's chosen?

If I am, then is a cedi enough for his unspoken,
daily meal,
place of residence – and any ordeal he may
encounter during the day?
Is giving this cedi such a big deal?
Will I get a receipt?
A seat at his graduation from the streets?
For me to shout and say,
"Hey! I contributed to you surviving defeat!"
Chale wote kraa, onhyɛ bi

Should I give a cedi to the kid on the street?

Light turns green
Cedi is given for free
Smile is returned as a form of receipt
Amazing, for I was trying to be discreet
Yet smile erases all conceptions of deceit
Will I see him again?
Will he be educated?
Is the money going to be used for water as he
asked?
Is it going to his master?
Is he hoping to be adopted by a half cast?

I'm now a beggar for answers
To a story I funded
A story with a tomorrow,

I will never know

BAT GIRL

I don't like my bed
My dreams gave up, broke its wings and wrote
these things
My dreams plucked its feathers for me to lie on
For me to sink my head on this fake comfort
Whilst the plumber in the afterlife, connects
my tears to pain

Walls have ears
but mattresses have eyes and fears to feel
emotions
They can feel when a pear becomes rotten

My pear became rotten

The bed knows this but says nothing
Says nothing because it … saw what the Pear did
It saw what it hid

I can't trust him

My daddy loves me
My daddy loves me yet sat on the bed
He sat on the bed looked at my broken dreams and
dismissed the story about the Pear
He said it was just a bear
A cuddly teddy, nothing I should fear
That my mind was just playing tricks on me

He couldn't see my nightmares
or didn't want to because,
the bed cushioned his perception
Making him reject my grief
It cannot be trusted
My dad too

I thus slept on a mat on the floor,
and for some weeks, I forgot that the two were
cousins

Pear again visited me
Visited me with his rottenness
Confirming that there was no cushion to ease
the pain
I felt the cold floor and watered it with tears
as prayers to bloom through the concrete and
bear a different fruit
Bear a fruit to witness this nightmare being
streamed for all to see

Why don't any of you stop what is going on?
Do you enjoy what you see?

Bed, I held your leg for help,
but all you did was sleep on me
I thus tried standing to sleep in the corner of
my bedroom
but ended up running away in my dreams
Only to end up lost in tears and
found by my bed
Who always brought me back and reminded me of
our secrets

I thus decided to sleep like a bat

So with the help of a skipping rope
and the hook that the ceiling fan used to
hang on

I lay my bed

and slept

This time I had no nightmares
This time I cried no tears

In the air,
Pear couldn't use his magic mirror to turn
things around and release another EP of
rottenness

144

In the air,
the problem and solution are closer than they
appear

Both the problem and solution
are sleeping on the woman

Today however, she sleeps like a bat

Alone

Because she is tired
Tired of being slept on

Poet's Notes

The fruit pear in this poem is a metaphor for rape. Both pear and rape contain the same letters. The idea here was to talk about a situation and hiding the problem in plain sight. Just like the rape stories we hear from victims.

It is interesting to read this poem and read it again to discover how that concept was missed. Wherever the word "Pear" is used, it is referring to rape. This is exactly what victims go through sometimes. I pray we do more to support victims to prevent them from destroying their lives.

No victim should endure additional pain because no one listened and believed.

POT LOVE

I want to be the pot that gets you high
The lingerie that makes you lie
The situation that makes you…
Hi there,
Sister let go of your breath
You were looking for a brother not shy
I think I passed the test
6 ft dark skinned, I could tell you the rest
But I like you to experience the detail
It may make you…sweat!

Could we hold hands some time?
We could start with fingers
Pinky over pinky to let our blood linger
We could take a walk down the street and I'll
sew you a singer
I know you didn't understand that line
My lines define, the fate of our first kiss
Call me glass, you are wine
For you make me tip - see
Not tipsy close to drunk but you see,
I have to tip my glass, in order for that wine
to pour
I'm sprung
I got T-pain
Meaning I brew our love like tea - but for days
So when I don't see your face - my heart aches
It provides a beat
My soul is the bass
And in case you were wondering
who the star of this show was,
It's you
Because your love is the song that keeps me
warm and gives me happiness

Not for one
But for two

MADNESS OF GREATNESS

Four claps could be heard at the seaside
10 km away from where Kwame lay
The sea shore and its waves sent a rhythm
through his ears as he lay in his bed
He was unable to sleep,
for he was confused as to why he heard these
sounds
Sounds from far away

Auntie Akorkor was 20 minutes away by the
bicycle his grandfather left him
She was complaining to her husband about the
meals that the children were supposed to eat

"Why should the children have one plantain
instead of three?", blurted Auntie Akorkor

Why am I listening to Auntie Akorkor's
conversation with her husband?
Kwame thought about this with eyes wide open in
disbelief

He could now hear a dog barking at a cat
climbing a wall
She had stolen a piece of fish the dog had set
for his meal
The claws signature on the walls as the cat
climbed
created a screeching sound that caused Kwame
to squeeze his face like a lemon being searched
for juice

Confused, he sat up
For the sounds kept rushing in

At the beach side where his brother worked,
a fight had sparked fiercer than the fire that
illuminated the battle

A battle of two fishermen over a woman
uninterested in the overweight fighters
The sound of sweat on muscles, slaps as they
wrestled,
the heaving, panting, alongside the potbellies
swinging,
created an unattractive sight that disgusted
Kwame so much,
that he covered his ears with his sleeping
cloth

But how can I hear what's happening at the
beach?
Am I being possessed?

This and more stressed and frightened Kwame

Was this what Grandpa told me about before he
died?
Was this what Grandpa meant by I was destined
for greatness?
Or am I …

losing

my mind?

Poet's Notes

*The inspiration for this poem stems from the
fantasy novel Across the Nightingale Floor, the
first book in a trilogy titled, Tales of the
Otori by Lian Hearn. The Novel is about a young
man blessed with special gifts due to his
lineage and his survival.*

DUNA 5.0

This is the back story of the background
The back story that compounds interest in the
shape of mounds
That weighs and values more than pounds
The back story that gives bass and sound
Takes space and crowns
Was rated by adjectives as the ace of nouns
The cake is found, its case is sound
This is the back story that turns men to hounds

We are talking about the latest national
treasure
An asset with a very big A-K-47 of back power
Power with magazines of jiggle causing men to
stagger at its perception
A perception whose background commands
attention at sight
This is a weapon of mass disturbance
Emotional noise which causes the male species
to perform calculations on many unnecessary
things
All in an effort to comprehend its
circumference

I stared at her butt
Orbiting it the whole day like a moon on
Jupiter
I imagined the thickness, softness, density,
whether both cheeks weighed the same
and what methodology one could employ to
ascertain each's mass
Like a Roman soldier, I attended its mass
services
As an Ass…trologist, I observed and deduced,
that this beauty wasn't just massive

It had bounce
Black canon ball heaviness
The likes that destroy ships

and men floating above sea level
Black canon ball heaviness merged with the
bounce of Spalding basketballs
My eyes turned to pinballs,
bouncing everywhere I sniffed a wiggle
Interesting see-saw mechanics were employed
to cause the adjacent cheek to rise
with trampoline spring like smoothness
when the other cheek had reached its desired
level

Mmmmmmm

The effect was mesmerizing like two buoys on
water allowing the waves of life to dictate
their up and down movements
My eyeballs were in sync with the up and down
It was perfection
I was spell bound in the aura it held me
I often felt it was more than I could handle
One cheek even was insurmountable in my opinion
What operating system was running this
exquisiteness?
I believe it's runs on a dual core processor
with 32gig of Round Ass Memory, 16gig per cheek
I upgraded from standard definition
to 4K HD to monitor this shapeliness

Jaws of men shall fall
Sunglasses are required in order to view its
radiance without being rude
This is the test that proves you are a dude
A true - BACK side story whose creation is
shrouded in mystery
Like an onion,
this shape will cause tears to fall throughout
history
Not of pain but of bliss
To have viewed and not missed
What I term a significant update in the world
of bums

Like a mouse, I will continue to follow this
cheese

This is the back story of the background
The back story that compounds interest in the
shape of mounds
That weighs and values more than pounds
The back story that gives bass and sound,
takes space and crowns
Was rated by adjectives as the ace of nouns
The cake is found, its case is sound
This is the back story that turns men to hounds

So if you're with me Gentlemen
let's raise our glasses and cheer the crown
Hailing, the latest queen

Duna 5.0

BLACKNESS

I wasn't called out of the blue
I was called out of blackness
Because of my skin color,
they think that I'm tactless
They see my emotions,
equate it to darkness
So I take their ill will
And turn that ill will into success

I listen more nowadays
And I talk less
For whenever I spoke in the past,
it felt like a trumpet
Going berserk at a concert,
going to church in a short skirt,
making a sinner a convert,
making sinning a conquest

No music, no harmony, soul,
just tragedy trying to console weakness
So we're out of control

We are illegitimate,
for deep down they know
that we are superior
They confuse us with their culture
Convince us that we are inferior

That's ostensible
A word they formed to make them look sensible
Making the truth appear as fake news
turning us into the expendables
It's ironic,
How is Africa the one that is dependable?
Paying all sorts of monies for resources
indispensable
It's funny,

I thought we did black magic

How did the white man get us to neglect
ourselves and forget that we are black?

What happened to Juju?
What happened to Voodoo?
Why couldn't we use this magic to get rid of
them, save ourselves and get our country back?

Our muti is weak – and the juju is wack
We need to reset our minds, stay alive,
use what they used on us to get our power back

It is called brain washing
Science and God, mixed with greed
It brought us strange fortune

Knives, beads, mirrors, rum, guns, for what?
Slaves, babes, chains, gains
No respect for black man
Even by the black man
So black man, now move forward
Move towards, the light at the tunnel
Move onwards, from hate and pain,
don't complain, make a way, make it rain
With thunder and lightning
Use your mind to do the fighting
Free your mind from all the chanting
Change your nothing into something

NOT ALL

Not all wishes come true
Not all treasure is silver and gold
Not all truth will be told
Not all truth will be bold
Some will be sold
Some will be old
But nevertheless, not all truth will be cold

Not all glitter is gold
Not all people are bold
Not all people change
Some prefer to be strange

Not all wounds are visible
Not all lies are dismissible
Not all moves are permissible
Yes, not all guys are kissable

You see not all birds fly
Not all girls are shy
Not all friends, say hi
And not all enemies, say die

Not all are meant to stay
Not all life is left to fate
Not all failure is a mistake
Not all mistakes, amount to disgrace

Not all choices are bought
But all choices come at a cost
Not all Christians believe in the cross
Outside of Star Wars, people believe in the
force

To comprehend effects, study the cause
To understand, one must pause
Not all who wander are lost
Not all lost, is a loss
Not all days are equal

Not all humans are people
Not all movies have sequels
Maybe all stories have prequels

Not all deals are fair
Not all treasure is rare
Not all storms bring despair
Some come, to make the path clear

Not all guys are players
Not all girls are slayers
Not all looking are seekers
Not all opportunists are reapers

Not all men are sorry
Not all girls are stories
Not all stories are in books
Not all who steal are crooks

Not all anger is bad
Some smart people, are mad
Some happy people, are sad
Some mothers, are dads

Not all black people are criminals
Not all police, are cynical
Not all white people are racist
Not all crime turns into cases
Not all classrooms have four walls
Not all men, have balls
Not all beds, have pillows
Not all tea is milo

Not all guys want sex
Some want, what is best
But not all girls can see
Mr. Right when he is kneeling at their feet

Not all questions are answered
Not all serving are backward
Not all fights will stop

Not all truth, is bought

Not all, are created equal
It doesn't mean, we are not the same
We all however, have the power
To make the world a better place, each day

BROKEN CRAYONS

I hate broken crayons
Their rebellious outlook naturally selects them
to be outcasts
Their broken nature makes them less than ideal
to create masterpieces

But masterpieces are broken

Each stroke of genius separates color from the
crayon
Kidnaps its luster and gentrifies its existence
So though broken, value speaks highly of the
misfortune
Like money in a gutter

Many of us are precious stones
Hidden deep in the earth we are birthed with
potential
But the time has not come for your potential to
be mined
For you to shine
For you to find
That the world is beautiful

Sometimes the one that finds you
does not know your value, so disrespects you
Treats you with so much hate and wickedness
that you begin to hate yourself

But broken crayons still color

No amount of hate and evil, except death
Can prevent you from coloring your world as you
choose
So pay no mind to the one trying to break you
Foster a mindset to thrive in unforgiving
situations
It may break you
Take you through the tracks of life

You will feel cold, you will feel the cracks of
ice
Nice, is not something we are promised
Pain on the other hand, is something life will
vomit
It will hurt and stain you with fear
You will share with others your tears

So don't be afraid
For pain is something that goes away
Like a window, it opens for the wind to carry it
away
So don't worry about your past or how broken it
is
A seed has to be cracked before a plant opens
and lives
A crayon may be broke - but pays his taxes with
time
Hope is an ingredient that fastens to time

So do not lose hope
Don't lose your cool
The broken crayon will color when the time is
due

When it does, the breaker himself will see the
jewel
Acknowledge that there is beauty in brokenness
too
And just like crayons, we are all in the same
box
Different, unique, broken and lost
Coloring our very own, masterpiece
Coloring our masterpiece, as we choose

THE QUEUE

I woke up at 3 in the morning
to go stand in a queue
If that statement doesn't bother you, well, stand
in a queue
As I got to the queue,
there was already a queue
Human beings, chairs and stones well positioned
like a screw
There were others standing
in line for others at the queue
I didn't mind, for it's something
that I knew they would do
But seven at a go is a bit
of a stretch at a queue
Especially, when the rest of us
came early to the zoo

I'm in shorts, a t-shirt
and slip-ons, as my shoe
That's stupid, for mosquitoes
are also in line for their brew
It's early morning, I guess I am tom brown with
the dew
Suddenly people were cutting the line at the
queue
As if those of us behind
would take this nonsense at a queue
Pulses flared, words were exchanged and there
was a quarrel at the queue
Unfortunately, there was no referee to decide
at the queue
Friends were made, along with enemies at the
queue

Patience wrestled with time and common sense at
the queue
Sewed his seeds of tolerance - but frustration
grew

Hours later, the officials arrived with their
crew
After hours of standing, I was kicked out with
my shoe
I came too late was the reason I was outed from
the queue
Pleading and begging by neighbors,
got me back into the queue

I was processed but had to come the next day -to
a queue
Waited another couple of hours to be attended
at the queue
After all this, I have wasted my time at the
queue
Skipped work for nothing but to get a tan at the
queue
Why can't I use Ghana Card to vote?
Please give me a clue
For this whole process is sick
Like someone with COVID and the flu

It's messed up

For many live for the queue
Smart politicians can't work a way to ease up
the queue
With technology and internet, we still got a
queue?
The same one, nothing shorter?
Someone is playing with my mood

Are you still in a queue?
Can you even leave the queue?
Maybe not
I'm hoping for hope to come through
Save the day
Replace pain
and ease up the queue

Poet's Notes

*I wrote this poem after going through the
frustrating two-day process of getting my Ghana
card which as of May 2021 I have been unable to
use for anything worthy of the card. When I say
two-day process, I literally mean two days which
is honestly from about 4AM to 5PM. It's
ridiculous and shameful that we can't use all
our intellect as a nation to make this process
quicker.*

PEP TALK

Laziness doesn't look good on you, so please,
don't try to wear it
Hard work fits better but you do it a
disservice
You prioritize the wrong things, so miss out on
the best deal
You're focusing on things that won't provide
your next meal
The watch you are wearing is nice, but I think
it's dysfunctional
I don't think you understand what it means to be
punctual
You don't need high heels to get you into high
places
Neither do you need Facebook, to meet new faces
You're interested in chases
You're a dog fixed on a bone that's a mirage in a
cage
You're stuck on a page
Stuck on the last sentence, you're stuck in a
daze
Forgetting there's more to find, there's more to
engage
You're free to be polygamous
Free yourself from religion and realize the
peace and truth that the songs of God speak
about
But freedom has boundaries
So be careful of your actions
Make sure they don't cross the line and get you
into acting
Scenes you don't want to do, or you'll suffer
consequences
Confidences vary when freedom crosses the
contrary perception
Realize that life is an infection
The only cure is to live it, so don't worry about
your reflection
For it will change repeatedly

So live on a high
And treat yourself with nothing bad but be a
surprise,
of good fortune
Push your limits and push for knowledge
That's your porridge, drink it and get
acknowledged
And when you're all alone,
be honest to yourself
Understand that everybody in this world needs
help
For we are all infected
If you're alive you are not rejected
If you feel that way, you're about to get
yourself defected
Commit suicide, we do or die
Don't cheat the game with suicide
Because the game got tough - or you are
suffering more than Jesus when alive
And I don't mean to trivialize, depression or
sadness
I just think that there's more help these days,
amidst the madness
So don't sell yourself short
Your life is destined for gold
Just do it you own way, brighten your road
Lighten your load of stress, keep fighting for
goals
Hard work never killed nobody
It just sharpened your soul

WHAT IF

What if Heaven did not exist?
Good or bad was just a hoax,
a post, a fake news campaign,
a boat on land gathering people who will
eventually turn into sand
Or a plane in flight causing stage fright
through turbulence
What if turbulence was fake news?
Not real
What if it's someone in the background pulling
strings to create fear?
Some say that's who God is
A mean guy who rains down earthquakes, typhoons,
hurricanes and rain to destroy people
What if that's not God?

What if that was us?
Our ancestors, our past actions that have
caused a butterfly effect

Repercussions

What if these so-called natural disasters are
not at all natural?
What if these are just consequences of us
taking over the forests
Building less trees, causing more smoke to go in
the air?
What if all that's not fair was supposed to be
so?
What if racism was supposed to happen?
Apartheid, Xenophobia, the Holocaust
What if these things were necessary?
Like a button needed to keep that shirt
together or that pair of trousers on a waist
What if all this is just waste?
What if there is no meaning?
What if it's all meaningless?

It is
For we carry none of our earthly possessions
and feelings along with us when death arrives
at our doorstep
We tie a corset, around our reality turning it
into an illusion
Believing our waistlines are smaller than they
actually are
The corsets act as filters or masks hiding the
reality
Fooling the receiver of sight
Turning perception into might
If all is indeed meaningless
What is the purpose of life?
Is good or bad even relevant
Is there a reason to delight?
What if we are in search of answers?
But the answers have already been given
Some accept, some question
And in that journey, they learn a lesson

What if we do not accept the truth?
What if we reject the proof?
Does it mean life is pointless?
Or are we living, in denial?

SELFISH

I sell fish
But I no wan sell fish
All the other kiddies, no dey sell fish
They laff my body, say I dey smell fish
They give me nickname, that I be "Selfish"

I sell fish
But I no wan sell fish
I do it for Mama
Mama go to circus
She paint her face; she juggle for circus
I miss my school and struggle, just to sell fish

Papa lef mama
But not to sell fish
He travel far away
Rather to catch fish

Now I grow
So I start to catch kiss
The feelings I get
Be sweet pass red fish
Mama see kiss
She ask why I catch kiss
I tell am say Mama,
Because I'm selfish

FIRST KISS

You were my first kiss but now I call no more
Last Tuesday I met the ice cream guy who sold us
our first ice cream as a couple
It's funny how I remembered him
It's funny how I remembered why we bought the
ice cream in the first place
How we slipped into a corner to try this silly
but exciting idea simultaneously

Your laugh was ...
Naughty
And yet,

I loved the danger you imposed that day

Now I don't know how I could forget the danger
and joy you bring to me
How I neglect your calls to me

I see them
Honestly, sometimes I am just too busy to call
back
Other times, I am afraid of getting caught back
in the fairytale atmosphere you send me to

My serious life doesn't have time for you
They say you are a worthless distraction
I say you feed my creativity
But who needs that these days?

You are beginning to look like that girlfriend
I wished I spent more time with
You are beginning to look like a side chick
making a comeback to be the main chick

But that's only because, you were the main chick
The family just didn't accept you
Their feelings upset you
And here I am now feeling lonely

Lorgorligi Locomotion   Hondred Percent

Debating on whether I should accept,

you

WHILE

I haven't free styled in a while
Haven't performed off the top of my head in a
while
Haven't pulled words and verbs out of the air in
a while
Matter of fact
I have not had an affair in a while

I just caught you off guard,
I haven't done that in a while
You girls are beautiful,
I haven't seen that in a while
I just saw some big boobs, so my brain froze for
a while
Can I have your number?
This poem will be done in a while

I try to act all righteous but sometimes I'm a
jerk for a while
If I offend you don't worry, it will only be for
a while
Your lips look nice, can I kiss you for a while?
I was just playing but you got excited for a
while
Let me sit for a while, sober up awhile
I drank too much wine so I may be tipsy for a
while
MJ's, "Don't Stop 'Till You Get Enough",
was playing in the back for a while
That's funny,

even MJ was black for a while
Let's pay respects, to the legends for a while

Let's pour a drink for Biggie and Tupac for a
while
Thank God for giving us Castro and DMX for a
while

Now Whitney, yeah, she could hold a note for a
while
DJ please play me, "My Love Is Your Love", for a
while

I think I am sober now but that will only be
awhile
I just ordered some red wine
which will come around in a while
This chick by me is fine and I want to dance in
a while
But she is talking too much so I have to drink
for a while
Her jokes are not funny but they will be in a
while
This red wine is cheap, it will get to work in a
while
And if it doesn't, I will pretend to laugh for a
while
'Cos I need this one dance to be like Drake, for
a while

2021 is here but it will only be awhile
Midnight comes everyday but it only lasts
awhile
RIP Ebony you did your thing for a while
So let's cherish those memories, that last more,

than a while

INTELLIGENCE BREEDS CONTEMPT

They say contempt is a witch doctor you visit
when the world pins you to the ground
A witch doctor who lives in the jungle and
wears a crown
A crown of teeth, bones and animal skins painted
in the blood of sacrifices
Sacrifices of wants and needs of the people

They say the witch doctor is evil
The kind of evil that,
slits your throat with a cloak
and proceeds to slit your sensitive organs
for shege reasons
Putting the slit organs in your neck
to wreck your fashion sense

But I see intelligent people

The so-called educated and ivy leaguers
Visiting this Professor Doom for answers
Answers that they've been searching for and
could not find
So their desire,
their hunger for answers
Triggers their intelligence to move to new
heights
The height of contempt in the witch doctor

Contempt is a radioactive bioweapon
A bomb that explodes invisibly without a bang
and pow
Latching onto your soul like a blade to a plow
It makes your blood cold
Raises your shoulders spiritually
Elevates your perception of your status like a
balloon
So you'll think you are a big deal
But in reality, you are a small rubber object

173

Filled with the hot air of intelligence which
will eventually burst out
Or escape gradually,
till you become deflated, or ruined

Such is life when you are okay with magic
tricks and spells
But this is no wizardry of the heathen
This is the bread of intelligence which has
stayed out too long

Stayed out too long,
and as result

Developed mold

WHO WILL I PISS ON

I have lots to give
I am a rock giving birth to uncontrollable
water
My water source is infinite
I am young and feeling it
Feeling the vibe to put out fires

So where are these flames?
Where are these problems?
Where, are these names?

Disappointed, Not Good Enough and Worthless

Come drink from my spring and receive life

As I went about giving fire water to drink
I forgot that his bladder would get full
Fire will need to piss

So, as I put out the fires, the flames vanished
But new buildings emerge awaiting renovation
I now need to become a toilet to receive what I
have given
Not doing this will cause these buildings to
breakdown
Be demolished, with little hope of being built
again
Reluctantly, I drink this piss
Drink this contaminated liquid that has
filtered through their systems
I have thus been transforming from a rock of
water to a pissing bowl
In and out, unenthusiastically
Because I wanted to help people

But now I am on fire
The piss I drank has turned into gasoline and I
am burning
I pretended to be able to do it, but I can't

I pretended to not be tired, but I pant

I have helped all these people
But what about me?
Who will save me?

And who,

Will I piss on?

Poet's Notes

*This was poem was developed of writing prompt
in a room on Club House. The prompt was created
after someone in the educational sector spoke
about their struggles in helping kids in
school. This was me expressing their
frustrations through poetry.*

SOME WAY

Love is a complicated thing
It infects like a cold and brings two people
together
Unfortunately, I fall sick easily
And I think you are showing symptoms too

Undercover we hide our heart beats
Our heart speaks new waves of feelings
that characterize our behaviors as strange
Or in the more perfect tense...

Some way

Somedays this some way leaves our lips
sweet like ripe plantain
Other days it tears us apart to a point
where we can't contain
We can't complain
We just remain ...

Some way

Is it loves fault?
Is love spoilt?
Or are we fixated in a cult?

Sometimes I think her beauty fools me
Sometimes I think it uses me
Abuses my senses to dream of her future tenses
I just wonder if she shares the same feeling I
feel
This ...
Some way feeling

TO MY EXES

To my exes
You are more than just the 'bestest,
friends a man can ask for
You did more than just affected, my lifestyle
You redefined beauty into a lifestyle
Now I appreciate women because of you
You took my heart out on vacation
Sometimes we went over-celebrating
Our dedication to what we had was more than
just us dating
Never hating, a moment
Our love letters were our opponents
In the academic arena, they won often and
promoted
Our feelings and resolve
So when in the dining hall, our eyes kept
searching for whether we were eating or
involved
In eye contact or that, we were reading a letter
in a format
Designed to create butterflies in our tummies
I never ignored that

Each of you I treated very special
My respect for you individually was more than
rose petals on the floor
Never regretted a moment and never saw
happiness like I saw in your eyes when we were
on our tour

High school had a lot of rules
We broke most of them
Some of them single, some together
We got closer than our subjects
Our feelings were more than just objects
Curfew was our enemy making our moments,
loveless
And the prefects
Cupid haters with an agenda for debaters

Gossipers, I mean
They are paparazzi without the data of
photographic intel'
I fell for most of you hard
Some it took longer but was sweeter than kiss
felt

Breaking up was always painful, for I'm an
optimist
So I wanted to marry each of you but that sounds
just like an alchemist
Trying to turn metal into gold
That was like my goal
Guess I never won your cup
But you helped me turn pro
Now we are friends
The trust between us will never end
Your boyfriend maybe jealous
Sorry I can't pretend
Enough said

You are Queens who made me into a King
I wish for your happiness forever
Signed your ex, with a dream

MASIKO

Damba, Damba where art thou?
Damba, Damba where art thou?

Oh, there you are
Come sit by me
Tell me again how beautiful I am
Tell me I'm the smartest little girl
An angel
Tell me that bruise I got from playing outside
is not painful
Tell me you love me
Wait!

You always do

Every night I sleep
Every morning I wake
And throughout the day

Oh, Damba!
I love you

Damba, Damba where art thou?
Damba, Damba where art thou?

Its 2002
I've been kidnaped by your people
They say they are your resistance army
Fighting for you Damba
They beat me with a gun
Taking me not to your castle
But a bush
They killed a man in front of me
He was my neighbour
I am only 12 Damba!
Only 12!
If these are your people Damba
Why are they demons and not angels?

Damba, Damba where art thou?
Damba, Damba where art thou?

He opened my legs Damba
Said I was his wife
But I am only 16
Sweet dreams replaced by sixteen thrusts
Bust size perfect but a bit too much
Trust not needed plus he came too much
So I am pregnant and a teenager
Tell me, is this real love?

Damba, Damba where art thou?
Damba, Damba where art thou?

It will be 9 months soon
A son is in bloom
Yet I walk for miles in labour
And he ...
Dies too soon

Never will I know if his hair is like a broom
But I'll never forget the razor blade used to
cut my womb
There was no anesthetic
There was no you
I could not cry for my son
For that will be my doom

Son thrown away in the bin like tissue
There is not even a tissue to cry and say I miss
you
And even if there was
The world will miss you
For you will die because crying, is an issue

Damba, Damba where the hell are you?
Damba, Damba where the hell are you?

Its 2006 and I'm really sick
Abortion wasn't done properly

So I am aborting my wish, to live

Damba you have a life to give
Give it to me already
I already lost one kid!

Damba, Damba where are you?
Damba, Damba where are you?

You were in the nurse that helped me in Kenya
You were in the staff at the Embassy who got me
back home
It's been close to 6 years without you Damba
Now Masiko your love, is back home

Poet's Notes

*Masiko is a female Ugandan name that means hope.
Damba is a male Ugandan name that means boy of
peace. This poem is inspired by true life events
by a Ugandan girl who was abused by the Lord's
Resistance Army (LRA) and escaped.*

*The poem is a poetic retelling of the Ugandan
girl's experience. Damba is representative of
God. The poem is a conversation between the girl
and God on His love for her and her suffering.*

HOW DO I SEE YOU?

How do I see you?
Do you exist?
Are you human?
Are you an angel?
Are you a skirt?
Are you a bird?
Or are you, beauty?
Are you what every woman wants to call herself?
Are you amazing?
Are you intelligent?
Are you…

What is the word?

Are there words to define what you are?

Maybe not
Maybe, I should create a word
But that is absurd
For you are more precious than diamonds
What I view is more precious than water
Because with you not existing, I wonder what I
will drink

Maybe I need a shrink

Did I drink too much brandy the other night?
Are you Brandy?
Are you an aphrodisiac?
Making me feel feelings, revealing temptations,
dreaming vacations with bottles of cocoa
perfumes with models dripping in oil?

I don't know!
Or should I say, mi nyim
Are you something that can only be described in
Twi?

You see, your love for fufu complicates the
thought process of answering the question at
hand
Kind of like looking at Ewe booty and revising
for math

Are you a memory?

Did I play with you as a kid when I was young in
nursery?

I try to look back in my mind and remember your
face
Maybe in spirit we played with each other but
can't remember the space, the time, the place
Maybe I chased but can't remember the chase

Maybe you smiled, maybe you giggled,
maybe you even tickled

Maybe sometimes I hurt you because I am a boy
and I made you cry

Maybe that is why we are friends

Because I made you cry, and felt so bad
making it my aim to never let anyone hurt you

I've not been really good at that

I've tried my best but fail repeatedly
to stop man from hurting your heart

Which exists to persist on love, insist on the
above being the needed feeling of being
received

Funny enough, all you have ever been is deceived

Meanwhile, all you ever wanted to do is channel
your laughter to this world that swirls and
creates pearls, in the sea

I see you as a teddy bear

A teddy bear in a gift shop with lovely fur
The kind of fur that you want to hold and smells
like honey

Coming to think of it, it looks like honey

With an expensive price tag that can only be
bought with money

Funny

That is what you are

A honey teddy bear in a gift shop,
That wants to run away into my bag
and let the security man standing at the door
arrest me

Because...

I stole you

FLOWER CHILDREN

Children are like flowers
They are prettier than roots and a cherry on
top of the cake of life
They are pleasing to the eye and the desire of
many
Their beauty often hides their journey
People and elements are involved and
responsible for their blossoms
They both share a likeness to possums
For failure to access the teat,
the lifeline to a young possum, spells doom

We obsess about what we see and not what we
can't
So forget that like flowers, children are
connected to branches and roots
To reach heights, there is always a struggle to
find water, sunlight and nutrients
A battle to create a conducive environment for
growth

The flower is a smile, a moment, a memory
A space of adorable time spent with loved ones
But maintaining a child's happiness involves
hard work
As a parent you are the root constantly
searching for nutrition and a climate to grow
Your desires must be pure
Your will must be tenacious and ready for
battle
For the things you search for will not be
offered without sacrifice

Wars are fought daily to enable the growth of
children
Often with yourself as the enemy
So when you see a child smiling, don't assume all
is rosy
For thorns garnish the stem of a rose bud

A truce may be called to see a child smile
but don't mistake that for meaning the war is
over
The will to create beauty is never enough to
sustain it

So before you decide to be a parent,
ensure you are not holding on to trouble
Fighting or battling with demons that can leave
scars
Scars that produce hurricanes
Destroying your seed and their generation
Mend the parts of your past that cause you to
burn souls

Don't desire a flower
when your garden is soaked in kerosene
yearning to roast coals
For beauty is fragile and has weaknesses
Innocence, can be turned into a biological
weapon
So understand the laughter of a child
and what creates them
Desire to sustain them
Honesty is a good fertilizer to breed and
maintain them
So dig deep and earth it out

Mend your garden before you ever decide to
breed flowers
For children are meant to blossom into orchids
Not wilt away six feet deep…on coffins

SHE WAS A PRAYING MANTIS

That was quick
Yet, the taste of satisfaction I yearned for
escaped
A part of me wants to smile and let out a
witches laugh
But I seem spell bound by the scattered limbs
and the cracked screen of the iPhone I envied
minutes ago

Was my curse an accident?
To be honest I didn't believe my wish for her to
meet her demise would occur so quickly

Was this my doing?
Which devil did I pray to for this accident to
come alive
I am not even the spiritual type, but I feel so
guilty right now
I am shocked by my internal sentiments
My mouth is still open, and I am on my knees
Flabbergasted and welling with tears for a
woman I called my enemy

Our love relationship as enemies was more
turbulent than that of fire and insecticide
Insecticide I chose to not use because I did
not see danger screaming till it was too late
This insect weaved her way into my life and
befriended me when I was at my lowest

I confided in her
Treated her like the sister I never had
She loved me all right
But like a praying mantis, cut my head off at
the height of her love

She slept with my husband and caused a bitter
divorce that drove me ballistic
Now all that feels like yesterday

Unimportant
I should be planning a celebration but instead
I am sad and a bit guilty

Did hate do this, or was it just her time?
I shake the guilt and broken glass of my skirt
Slip her iPhone into my handbag and walk away
looking for my phone technician's contact at
Circle

If he can get this iPhone working again
It will compensate my suffering
A selfie and appropriate hashtag
will be uploaded soon

IS THIS STORY OVER?

We started this story with a perfect ending in
mind
We convinced ourselves that the path was clean,
hearts were good and that the souls of men,
were made of innocence

Along the way however,
the house that we built with dreams and
sentences
begun to fall apart

It started with the door handle
Followed by the lights, then the door
The wall finally broke and pipes burst
Finally, the roof caved in
The roof caved after months of using excuses
as duct tape and band aid to hold the house
together

This wasn't the story we wanted to tell
Our yellow brick road didn't lead us to The
Wizard of OZ
Things have fallen apart, and like Achebe,
we have decided to hang our Okonkwo,
our dream, our goal

Our story

Because we couldn't tame the wind
and fit it into a bottle
we decided to pretend it never happened
Like dust swept under a carpet
The problem never goes away
The story remains
The bricks used in building that house
don't have the privilege of growing limbs to
move
We possess such power
We just might have to adjust

192

if we want the story to be told

The architecture and paint may have to change
We may opt for fewer windows and a single door
A see-through roof to talk to the stars and the
sun
We may even change the location

Because

Things change

And our plans like men
have a mind of their own

Predictable stories are boring
We would not read books we know the ending to
So why are we surprised and let down
when our stories embark on a rollercoaster?
Why are we so upset at tragedy befalling us
that we choose to quit?

It's a page turner
An opportunity to experience life on a
different dimension
You don't need to be ready
You just need to accept that stories behave
this way
and never give up on yours

So I ask again

Is this story over?

RELATIVES

Just because they are relatives
doesn't mean that they're close
Blood may be thicker than water
but relatives sometimes are foes
Relatives sometimes approach
you with intention to draw blood
They're not interested in your shelter
but rather to keep you in the mud

I've seen brothers curse each other
Mothers kill their spouse
Fathers rape their own daughters
all while living in the same house
It's not because of religion
but more to do with sin
I am not my brother's keeper
That's the feeling from within

They say crime does not pay
In the long run, some may say
But to the abandoned young man,
that truth does not sway
For when all was lost
crime gave him a family of thugs
And though they plunged him into darkness,
there, he found love

For someone was willing to die for him,
to side with him,
didn't care whether he was wrong or right,
I side with him, for he is my brother

That was the justification needed
Despite a wrong seeded no apologies were
pleaded
Yet such blind loyalty is hard to find,
in hearts defined to take up such loyalty
Rather they multiply, selfishness and greed
So much their hearts reply

Gimme more! Gimme more!
So the ties resign

Love is a misunderstood term
An undercooked verb
A good herb underutilized
A power hook served by the good and bad

Good or bad may do you mad
Without patience and forgiveness,
that love may screw you bad
Because some of us are not ready
to take up such responsibility
Our community suffers, because elders have
immunity

So where's the love?

Where is that 1st Corinthians, 13 verse 4-8?
Does it correlate
With our so-called Christianity?
Rather we fornicate
We complicate hypocrisy
That there's no debate
Just our way of showing love
We point out all mistakes
We say we are family
but that's just more mistakes
For most times it's pretend
Never a defend, or weekend of commitment
Our connection has weak ends
Cause just because we are relatives
don't mean that we are close
Blood may be thicker than water
but relatives sometimes are foes
Relatives sometimes approach,
you with intention to draw blood
not interested in your shelter
but rather to keep you in the mud

IF MY MASK WROTE A POEM

This is a one-night stand where what we say
shall not be seen
You are a machine whose job is to use and
dispose of me
Kick me out after I saved your life

You publicize our relationship
But hide your feelings towards me
So no one sees the smiles, sadness, anger and
bliss
I provide to you
Though we share kisses
We share blessings and sneezes as well

You're so selfish that food separates us
You discard me and bring me back into your life
after you have been nourished

There are others that you use as well
Each of us gets to ride the palanquin
of your lips and nostrils

When I am not on, I get very jealous
Yet my jealousy is useless
Invisible like the virus that caused us to
connect
I regret these feelings that exist in my fabric
Regret the sentiments of being desired and the
rejection

But such is the nature of our relationship

And by tomorrow, I will be of no use

LAMBO

She stands on the sidewalk
five steps away from the lamp post
Ten steps away from the road where she hopes a
Lambo'
Will drive by with a bye-bye proposal
To say, bye-bye
To the nice guys,
that hold on to her nice thighs
They give high fives to her back side,
I say that's why,
she dreams of a Lambo'

She prays to God and hopes he gives her a Rambo
I pray he comes with ammo
To kill her pain
For this next guy doesn't know her name
Even though it hurts her,
that is the game
That's the transaction
It requires no names
Just private parts and brown big sixes
But she plays a dangerous game of ludo
Chance is not enough
so sometimes she involves juju
Those big sixes will neither buy her freedom
or a way home
Her heart is replaced with something harder
than stone
So she doesn't understand love
She stands outside a lot
so she understands bugs
Mosquitoes, the female kind
They are out for blood and she for cash
So they compare strategies
Fake orgasms pay the bills
Mobile money is necessary
So she has four yams like a yam seller
with each of the networks
It's called customer service

She prays as she goes towards a prospective
client
Asking for forgiveness and security at the same
time
He says she is beautiful
She knows it's a lie
But she doesn't get compliments often
So she takes it
She fakes it
The laugh, the accent and shape wear
Her mentor advised that she represented herself
this way
It is working tonight

It is late and Mr. Compliments wants it fast
He suggests the car as the bedroom
She suggests a road where she last used
Inconspicuous with no lights
She preps her client for service and moved in
to deliver
It was almost a happy ending
Till she heard a knock on the glass and saw a
light
She has been busted for entertaining
He has been caught in the heat of the moment
But the doors were locked
Mr. Compliments wanted his monies worth
The officer kept knocking the glass
Mr. Compliments motioned to the officer that he
was coming

The next 30 minutes involve Mr. Compliments
negotiating with the officer and paying him off
It didn't bother him, for he didn't have to pay
her
She was pissed because she just got ripped off
On top of that, she has to sort the officer out
or else find herself at the station

He gave her two options

Cash or a free ride?
Her ego had already been scarred
So she declines
Just paid him off and walked back
Back to her usual spot waiting for the Lambo'
She was pissed
But the next customer could care less
She stores her anger in the cloud for when she
gets home
Adjusts her clothing and reapplied her makeup
This was not a breakup
Just a temporary setback
in the business, of the day

DEEP

I like to be deep but not all the time
Sometimes I like to recline and rewind in my
mind
Take a chill pill, procrastinate, not learn or
design
Spit a freestyle and not worry about who hears
or decides
whether it is dope or not
I have been referred to as a coconut
Black outside with white spots like a polka dot
You may not get it but what they mean is, I'm not
black enough
Because I don't eat waakye or speak Twi, I am not
Coke enough?
Well screw coke and their caffeine
I am coffee and I am sweet enough
Sometimes that's the attitude you ought to get
when you're deep enough
But even this deep,
sometimes I discriminate or hate or alienate,
I have to eliminate, my stubbornness
Gotta' stop seeing folk as commoners
Each of us is special
Yes, there is a lot more to us
So respect my opinion - and I will respect
yours
Remember there are limits to what's right and
wrong
But the world nowadays has become too sensitive
So wrong is alright, right is kinda' tentative
Real fouls ignored; petty fouls called
Too many chickens calling foul indoors
Too many leaders not wanting to serve
Too many leaders just trying to swerve their
responsibilities
This is not limited to politicians see
In my humble opinion, we aren't working together
efficiently, as a human race
But right there is the problem we,

see life as competition
So we can't work together cordially
White race, black race, everything now is a rat
race
So malpractice sets in
I am not talking about a drug case
Human trafficking, rape and hate crimes the
inhumanity
All this in the 21st century? What a calamity
Churches now take consultation fees? Such
insanity
We are eroding the eco system
at the same pace as our morality

Globally, we can't even agree on global warming
They all went to school
but still we are blind to the warning
Morality is rare these days but try and find it
And when you do be brave, don't act so hard to
hide it
For you could be right and wrong at the same
time
so take time, when jumping to conclusions
for you can fall at the same time

Majority isn't always right, minority isn't
either
So how do we find the answers to our questions
and misdemeanors?
I don't have the solution, just know it's about
balance
So let me balance these words

With a moment of silence

QUESTIONS

They say the pen is mightier than a sword
But is it mightier than a smartphone?
Is social media a reflection
of who we are in our own zone?
Since the word rhymes,
is that why we don't care about our ozone?
Layer is a concept but,
do we apply it to our own shows?
I hear photoshop makes us perfect
So are we now imperfections?
Is everything nowadays
going to be decided by elections?
There are Decepticons among us
Can't we see the deception?
When you look in the mirror, tell me,
do you see your own reflection?
Because your profile pic' on social media says
different
Your stories, pics', snaps, tweets, all say
different things about you in real life
Who are you trying to please?
The selfies are too much, who are you trying to
tease?
Which doctor prescribed the tablets we use to
consume our media?
Is such consumption exposing us to some new
bacteria?
If Twitter is a bird, are we birds of prey in
the area?
Or mosquitoes sucking blood and just giving
people malaria?
For the symptoms are similar
Is fake news malaria?
Causing us to change the way we see things as
familiar
Why is, sex so familiar? Why are sex tapes
peculiar?
Why is the smart phone so personal
used to just capture exteriors?

Are our values changing?
Is the smartphone the new criteria?
Is social media coffee we get from the
cafeteria?
Is the smartphone the cafeteria? Caffeine the
bacteria?
Making us addicted, believing scams in Nigeria?
Are the cracks on the screen,
the pain we feel in the interior?
If so, are the cracks larger on the smart phones
in Syria?

We may be more connected,
but are handcuffed to the internet
Charged with electricity,
we treat each other with disrespect
Mobile prison cells,
may be causing us to be circumspect
But who is the prison warden?
Is it the ISP's and their intellect?
The questions on my mind,
are in gigabytes and terabytes
We started at floppy disks
and have evolved into a mega white
cloud of information,
globally accessible to the ever bright
Who sometimes use this power for evil
So I ask, is the world ever right?
I end this series of questions,
with the same one I started with
It may contain the answer,
or is maybe just the starter kit
If the pen is mightier than the sword,
is it mightier than the smartphone?
Then again, you can't turn a pen off
As you would, a smartphone

SKULLS & FIGURINES

Skulls and figurines dance on my tabletop
The skull's head is bigger
The figurine's fable lost
Both lost their meat; one is racist towards the
other
The skull is white and bold
The figure, black with luster
They both need each other
Yet hate each other with pride
Dancing to life's tune
Telling each other a lie

PRETTY WOMAN

She was used to not meeting the parents
The front door was only used late at night
with the kitchen door being her exit
depending on which relation or friend
was in the house in plain sight

Her profession required her to be prepared
to play hide and seek and jump over walls,
with the added benefit of sometimes
being taken to a hotel or guest house

She never understood the phrase,
"make up to break up"

Hers was always,
"makeup to makeup"

With attraction as a factor in her business,
it's amazing that she does not gym
On most days she is not slim
Sin is forgotten in her Bible every Sunday
like the other phone she has with that special
sim

She never misses church
Her prayer room is usually in bathrooms
Usually in tears
Occasionally popping pills to reduce stress,
headaches and her womb from growing a bump
Perfect candidate for inception
Contraception can be forgotten if the price is
right
In this trade, love does not exist
Even when it is expressed,
it does not fit
Tits and butts pave the way
What ifs, are not tolerated
Unless they are backed up by collateral
No wonder some call them bitches

Their territories are marked on the streets
Even though its night,
they are always on heat
Their filament of imagination is messed up
Cause even though every night they are screwed
tight
That bulb unfortunately never may give light

Magnetically they reason with 4 by 4's
Regret intercourse
Experience pain by force
With money being the tissue paper
with which they hope to pause, their life

The word virgin to her is like an old Nokia
phone
Her home is a ringtone which is not pleasant
and constantly keeps changing
Like the money she receives,
she is always exchanging
Learning dance moves to be entertaining
To ensure she doesn't get HIV, she is always
praying

Being pregnant is like catching a cold
No doctor needed
Home remedies, the pharmacy,
and behind the scenes chemistry,
will get rid of this cold fast
Before you know it,
she'll be back on the scene

Bipolar to an extent
Gemini with intent
For her name always changes in the evening
to reveal another person

A Dr Jekyll and Mrs. Hyde
Catering for a league of extraordinary
gentlemen
A pretty woman waiting for Richard Gere,

who I fear, is not available yet

The one who is forever around
is never given a fair - Chance

Life is but a glance
and pretty is not forever
I hope she finds herself
Before her life is through in this weather

THE CHURCHLESS

Nowadays I go to church less

The prayer there is too loud
So whenever I pray I feel helpless
I don't think God hears me
I fear the tongues spoken
cloud the air waves and my train of thought
So I am unable to let God know that I am hurting

There is no dress code
But the stress shows on Saturday evening,
when I look in my closet
Dismissing the attires that would make me feel
comfortable before God,
and rather go for what is acceptable before his
servants

I go to church less
because I have become subservient
to the congregation and church culture
just to get a pass to go to heaven

But which heaven?

This heaven I am paying for feels wrong
Feels typical
Feels torn

This heaven I walk on
walks on me
This heaven frowns on my hairstyle
and choice of music
Loves those who give more than those who give
less
They hate questions
Love to waste time
and stretch services blaming it on the
anointing
Guilt tripping people to let go of their cash

So I started to move back
Move away

Like a boyfriend
who just realized the pretty girl
with nice dance moves isn't exactly
wife material and is morally corrupt

I move away
but visit now and again hoping
Hoping that the love professed,
will be real

But I end up choking
Choking on a lifestyle that took me from
feeling worthless to nothing

Like a zombie I am
repeating and agreeing to the
hallelujahs and praises
Never asking myself whether
what I have is a true relationship with God

But how do I find the truth?
I thought the church was where
the good guys hang out
The choir sings to God and is a catwalk
to view sisters and brothers looking for new
masters

Pastors and ministers
speaking brother and sister language
seldom seek to help you find the answers
Rather they point towards things that make no
sense
And when called out, resort to prayer
which sounds more like distraction than a
solution

I feel more lost than found

And no one wants to listen
Christians feel entitled
and get offended when people disrespect them
Yet, disrespect other religions and cultures
all the time

That's a love I can't comprehend
A love that spends more time pointing fingers
than understanding

Feels like a weird way to go about branding
But it happens anyway
Billboards and posters by churches
flood the streets but God is not marketed
A fake look alike is put up as an attraction
with a message claiming to point followers
towards God .

So why not point them to God in the first place?
Why establish a man instead of Jesus as the
focus?
Sounds like misdirection
and that's why I declare myself churchless
and almost, giving up

Poet's Notes

One of the powerful things about art is its ability to express self. It is interesting how one's thoughts can be shared and resonate with people to eliminate the feeling of being alone.

I wrote this poem not because I don't go to church but to express what it feels like for those who have given up on church. It's also for those who don't understand why someone will chart that path.

Whatever position you stand on the topic of God, just know that He loves you. Don't let man show you how God is, experience Him for yourself.

TRUTH AND LAW

The truth and the law are not the same
The game makes the law a fame but became
constrained because the law had an affair with
a dame
Changing the game into a love affair
A love disturbed
A love returned
A love concerned? No
A love unconcerned with who gets hurt or not
As long as the law is upheld

The truth and the law are not the same
The truth is more complicated

I am a 32-year-old lawyer who dresses to kill
in a Mercedes C class
Climbing the class ladder all the way to first
class
I see ass and apply what I call the
cockstitution
Which enables me to cast that ass into my
personal episode of Law and Order
But my law is disordered
I am sophisticated
Intimidated only by money
Go to church for political and social reasons
I tag myself Christian
because it makes me look professional
But I am a walking contradiction
You see, religion is not welcome in my
profession
So don't bring God into the equation
because it confuses things

I have a moral code but often it lacks the
letter "M", turning it into an oral code
I am in oral mode
when dealing with a female that's desperate
Often attracting a 25% discount

And baby, that's on the bribe
Before your case is ever tried

No pro bono
I am a professional that listens to Bono
when I am driving my Mercedes solo
My charm is like Han Solo
My drink is Henessy
And when I choose
not to be an alcoholic, it's Sobolo

I work to eat
I really don't care about your situation
Only what the law says
You may think I am wicked,
obnoxious and a guy only interested in money

You are right

But there is a reason why I live like this

The truth is not a celebrity in the courtroom
because it's hard to believe
But when you take a closer look at exhibit "A",
you will understand why it is so
Because when you take away the "b-e"
and the "v-e" you are left with a l-i-e, a lie
That's why the truth is so hard to believe
but the lie on the other hand is received
Because you and I were never there
So even under oath the Bible never scares
Maybe the Quran should be used
to try and just repair
Or the judge should use a saw
instead of a hammer to pass judgement
Cut the gavel in half and see whether it tips
the scales
Or maybe we should scrape a new set of scales
from a new fish that does not smell

The truth and the law are not the same

The law is in pursuit of the truth
so needs the suit to trap the truth
Purrs softly - but won't hesitate to shoot
Doubt is the prostitute
The law uses her to navigate the truth
The law is in search of the truth
but sometimes more comfortable with the lie
Like a man in search of love
but more comfortable with a set of behinds
The truth is perfect
but we want a new design
One that has a shorter skirt and a body just
divine
And that's how we have the lie

The truth and the law are not the same

The law is just a frame
The truth is just the canvas
The truth is just the face
But sometimes faces wear masks
And when the truth, faces a mask and accepts it
What we have is a lie
And the frame, in all its beauty and glory
Cannot tell the difference

MAD LOVE CHEMISTRY

Our chemistry is so strong
we don't need to perform experiments
Love is not periodic so let's forget about the
elements
You have a heart of gold, so Egoli is
irrelevant
AU is in session
We are the only ones killing it
You're soft and you're malleable
Hidden but valuable
No bling needed even if you wear calico
Kalyppo sipping in the Bahamas
Chilling in pajamas
Debating over bonding less the drama
A hypothesis is not needed
Our love is not a hunch
So send Quasimodo back to the gypsy bunch
I have a crazy hunch
That lunch will take place on your lips
And I'll experience a chemical reaction
when I get a kiss
That is bliss and gray matter
Solved with Greys Anatomy
Between you and I,
that is just a prophecy
Lobotomy is not needed for our condition
It's crazy but I'm chemically imbalanced for my
decision
I'm stuck on repetition
Saying "I love you", 10 times a day
That's doubled, whenever you and I have a date

Our love is so hot
Touch my chest, I turn into chocolate ice cream
A chocolate nice dream
Right side tastes like Frankies
Left side Arlechinos
And since they were six shops apart,
you can call my six pack Oxford Street

215

And that's when you're coming from Danquah
Circle

You are the apple of my eye but with no serpent
That means when it's you and I you see my souls
surface
I didn't find you, so I fell in love on purpose
Because God chose you, so I'm not nervous
I'm never out of service
So you can always call for no purpose
This feeling is that which money can't purchase
I'm double Curtis
With a rep' I catch your smile like circus
Your laughter blesses me,
like sneeze and churches

I dwell in your embrace
Fantasize face to face sessions
what we have is destined not a mistake
To not love you is a disgrace
So I do it and chase
your smile everyday
Just to replace, my sadness
This love indeed is some madness
Keep driving me crazy
Keep giving me the gladness

Poet's Notes

This piece is more rap than poetry. There are however gems hidden that I want to draw your attention to.

In the beginning there is a line about gold, Egoli and AU. They are all related. I remember Egoli as a South African soap opera which meant, Place of Gold. Egoli is also an alternative name to South Africa by the Zulu's. AU is the periodic element for Gold as well.

The line about Frankies and Arlechinos is about two ice cream shops in Osu, Ghana on Oxford Street. Arlechinos stopped operating a while back, but they were six shops apart at the time.

The double Curtis phrase refers to the rapper 50 Cent. Two 50 Cents make 100 cents.

JOURNEY TO THE SLAUGHTER

We walked on the clouds
Clouds of white, bordered by mountains of black
Clouds of destiny, bordered by angels of
purpose
A purpose nurturing the grass and fruit of the
earth
This clouded road was beautiful yet difficult
to navigate

I was often lost in its beauty

So lost, that I sometimes fell off track
I fell into the valley and walked in its clouds
But these were clouds of dust
Clouds of betrayed trust
The horns on my head
matched my stubbornness in strength
My curiosity, matched the ass my master sat on
to lead

It's a lonely and ugly journey to walk alone
It's more satisfying to walk together
Together with my brothers and sisters
With the clouds and the mountains
gloriously marching towards our unseen destiny
With trust in a master, who is unlike us

The only problem on this road,
is that we are walking to the slaughterhouse
The journey is short and long
So regardless of the road chosen
we end up sitting and waiting for a bus
to take us to the other side

So will you walk alone or walk together?
Will you walk in joy or in misery?
The only way we live forever, is to live to the
fullest
So run,

Lorgorligi Locomotion   Hondred Percent

and let the wind, carry your immortality

NECK ACHE BACK ACHE

I love bicycles

I love bicycles because to move forward,
One must balance their fear of falling
with the excitement of the wind running into
your face

You balance life by taking a step forward
and rotating the wheels of time into the future
My future, turned my body, into a bike
My neck was the frame and my back the wheels
Taking me everywhere and nowhere

I ended up getting a neck ache
My neck ache turned into a back ache
Life wasn't sweet because I was the pan and not
the pancake
The two multiplied each other and made my neck
unturnable

I had to turn my body around for turning to be
credible

Socializing was legible
Medication unstoppable
Coupled with psychotherapy
My life is already horrible

The doctor tells me my spine is
turning spongy due to
sitting long hours and bad posture
Actually, I think it's because
I had a chip on my shoulder
The microchip on my shoulder
told me to purchase a good chair
and the pain will be over

It's 6 GHC to the dollar
Meaning my pain will be over in October

Now my lymph node is swelling in my neck
What the heck!
The dollar just went up and my surgery is set

Did I mention I am jobless?

That's right
I am not working

Just a student with a nice smile
who believes in miracles
And the miracle of the surgery was...

It did not happen

After 3 days of waiting in the hospital
Doctor walks into the surgery room
as I am high on gas and deemed the surgery
unnecessary

That miracle, cost me 5000 GHC without a single
cut

Fast forward to the near future
I got a job that made me work with a nice
computer
Neck ache turned to back ache
rode into my life again with a vengeance
This time, my right hand swelled up
I developed a love hate relationship with
trotros
for their bumpy rides and pain they caused me
The Orthopedic Doctor suggested I had
rheumatoid arthritis

What is that?

It sounded like arthritis with jewelry

That's me in denial talking

as the condition is stalking

I didn't want to accept it

It was just neck ache and back ache
Neck ache and back ache riding into my life
again
Stubbornness and pain confirmed
I was the pan and not the pancake
Eventually I accepted it
Like my boyfriend's bad habit of not washing his
plate
This however, came with cocktails
Lots of cocktails, with expensive price tags
We are talking Johnnie Walker Blue Label
type drugs that I required to keep my
functionality

Family members had a go at getting
rid of the condition that had jewelry
From prayer meetings to herbal medicine,
midnight water sprinkling,
I had been through it all

I wish my embarrassment was
compensated with a healing
Unfortunately, it didn't
But I know my family meant well

My confusion had now reached its climax
Suicide played with me like a game on an iMac
Pain abused me and used me as a pimp
attempting to sell me to suicide
And I almost gave in

If it had not been for the piece of paper
with the dreams I had 10 years ago,
I would have ridden neck ache and back ache
into the sea

Those were the bad days

When you look at me now
You can't tell that my mornings are messed up
Cold messes with my senses, so harmattan is not
welcome
Neither is sugar or meat in most instances

It helps me get by
Unless I tell you though, you would not know
I try to stay tough, I however can melt like
snow

This is the result of being high on life
But this is not drugs
And I am tired
So these days I take neck ache and back ache,
along with my fears
to balance this bike ride called, life

Poet's Notes

*This poem was my first commissioned piece to
bring awareness to people living with auto
immune diseases. It's a true story of a brave
lady in Ghana and her early struggles with
rheumatoid arthritis.*

*I was honored to have been given the
opportunity to learn about the condition and
applaud the efforts of many in Ghana who are
fighting to help others who battle in this area.*

I WILL GIVE YOU A NIGHT LIKE NEVER BEFORE

How many shots of vodka will it take
for this date to turn into the date
where you don't hesitate?

This is supposed to be what I call a "dick-
tation"
I provide a dick and you provide a citation
With your upper and your lower voices
I promise to make no noises
Don't give me choices
Just perform
But that's not what it looks like
Is happening

Girl you're drinking too much juice
You're supposed to be loose
Booze must run down your system
I have to have you before snooze
No cools
I'm not looking for romance
No blues
Just 2 Chainz and Weezy
I set the mood right and easy
Yet all the girl does is play with her coaster

The only reason why I talked to you
Is because you reminded me of a poster

FHM 2015 October
I don't have to know her
Want to get in like I want to get in a Rover
I'll show her

Girl, I have a diploma in remembering body
structures
I'm now a master writing dissertations
Of the sensations that a man feels when a girl
decides to give him a citation

And she is still drinking juice

Didn't you say you like sprite
Riiiiight

I go over to the bar
Order her a sprite
Add some ice
Then I, spike the tall glass with 5 shots of
vodka
Don't ask

Served sprite with some ice
In the night
She took a bite
What did she say?
NICE!

Now we are getting somewhere

Lap dance
Lap dance
Lap dance
Lap dance

She wants me
Her horny has been activated
She is getting agitated
"Let's go", she says
"Yes ma'am", I say

Pay the bar
Get the car
Play with her whilst driving the car
She is making those sounds
that make me want to go far

You must be wondering where I met her at

Shoprite
That's right

University chick who bumped
into me, chuckled and said, I like you
Slipped her number into my back pocket
and made a gesture for me to call her
I can't help it if I'm sexy

She texts me
After that we exchange numbers
Flirt wirelessly
Tirelessly, we enquire of each other's personal
details

And skip all that, for we are now in my parking
lot

She handcuffs me and says
"I want to do you right here in the car"

My eyes pop out with excitement
She pushes my chair back
Jumps on top of me and winds me up
Blind folds me,
Kisses me seductively for 40 seconds
and ties my mouth up whilst whispering

"I'll make you scream
but I don't want the neighbors to hear"

She was serious

I soon heard voices

Male voices

My pockets were searched
for my house keys, phone and wallet
I heard people getting into my house

If you have not figured it out by now,
I was getting ROBBED!

My dictation turned out to be an
invitation to thieves
Thieves who robbed me
whilst I sat in my own car

So all that she said was true?

And here I am shaking my head
Because the first thing she said
when I picked her up was this,

"I will give you a night, like never before."

KILLER HUNTER

Heart beatboxing hunting for emotions
Knives being sharpened looking for the point
Not going out to play, just looking for a game
Chasing an antelope but now I find a snake
I bow to the ancestors, I'm praying for direction
Photosynthesis, is aiding my connection
Stuck at an intersection, I gain a new
complexion
Greed changed my color, so I am in a new
direction
I am in the corner breaking taboos and
agreements
Achievements? Yes, chale I see them
I feed them
But now I sold their freedom ... for progress,
But is more less?
Trees bore plus me, I changed my re-quest
Full of pride, so I do not re-gret,
I do not re-flect
Eat the sweet first
Not worried about the bitter
for I didn't need sweat

That's an illusion

For I was hunting now I am killing
Messing with the balance now looking for a
shilling
I got the money but - look at what I am building
Something less glamorous than the forest that
was chilling

Regret sets in
Now I see the resemblance
I look like sin and still I made an entrance
My defense is, I was playing devil's advocate
But who was the lawyer in defense of my
Africans
I preached hypocrisy, on the pulpit

I got stuck in my own trap like the culprit
I didn't bring firewood home
I am traveling slow
A hare running from the tortoise
I'm traveling cold
My embarrassing soul, sold its clothes
so now it's naked
The rain now plays dirges,
on my naked being
I ate the fruit of greed
I cut our lives unknowingly,
still our hearts they bleed
I am no longer a hunter
But a terrorist indeed
Now the only person left to kill is ...

Me

BEING A GHANAIAN 101

Hello, my name is Professor Logoligi
A research fellow at the institute of Ghanaian
Identity

I have been tasked by the nation to take you
through a quick orientation on being a Ghanaian

It's a necessary exercise to ascertain
eligibility before we begin the paperwork for
your status as Ghanaian

Let's proceed

Let me teach you how to be a Ghanaian
Let me walk you through the process and
transform your mind to that of the African
Black Star
Let me equip you for success, let me toughen
your veins, let me show you how to lord over
this jungle insane

To be a Ghanaian one must be selfish
Your major goal in life is to be rich
To achieve this, dwell not on hard righteous
work
Be corrupt
Develop an abrupt nose
to sniff out opportunities
Be ready to line the pockets of necessary
individuals to buy yourself immunity
Forget about the community
Success is not achieved when one chases unity

This will involve ridiculous contracts,
a broken moral compass
And art skills to paint, bribe money as lunch
money to meet your goals
You'll cheat others of what they are due
whilst looking for gold

Exaggerating prices and charging gargantuan
fees
But like a hidden disease, this cancer shall be
internalized for free

To be a Ghanaian you must offset
this trait of corruption by appearing friendly
Use the term chale carelessly
Have optimistic phrases like, "God dey",
to encourage others
Always claim to be broke
But walk and talk like a boss unafraid to
unleash the threatening phrase, "Do you know who
I am?"
Say it with confidence – and speak like an
aristocrat with connections

That brings me to education
It is more important than going to heaven
Ensure your secondary school education follows
that of schools with class and prestige
You can further your education outside to climb
the career and success ladder with ease
Making the chip on your shoulder legitimate and
you proud, like a dada bee

How you accrue your certificates is your own
affair
Legitimate and illegitimate ways must be
utilized to clear the air
of any doubt the public may have in your
capabilities

To be deemed worthy of the title of Ghanaian
A course in criticism is important
This however, is not taught formally in
academic institutions
Before God, this will be your first religion
You shall criticize day and night and not,
I repeat, NOT do anything to make things better

Public institutions and situations like
traffic,
are key areas to critique daily
Soccer and the Black Stars are another
fundamental talking point
A worthy subject to showcase your critiquing
skills
Be ready also to criticize and make fun of
secondary schools and prepare a rebuttal to any
arguments
thrown as daggers to poke holes at your alma
mater

Being a Ghanaian means you must be
a member of a political party
The elephant or umbrella will do
Your function as a member is to ridicule and
stupefy anything the opposition suggests
Be armed to the teeth with history
History of their faults to be used
alongside your critiquing course
to render their arguments baseless and insane
You will be duly compensated in favor for this
loyalty regardless of the side you choose

This next trait akin to Ghanaian identity is a
treasured one
A double-edged sword of a trait, with the power
to solve and cause problems
The art, of taking things easy

Being lackadaisical
Simply learning to relax
Being fashionably late
See deadlines as pencil etchings that can be
erased
Don't take life seriously
The sun is too hot!
To execute this with flair, your humor must be
top notch
Laugh heartily and bluff

Throw the rhetorical pidgin phrase,
"abi you know?"
With a smile and have an excuse and joke on hand
to de-escalate heated situations arising from
your relaxed demeanor

It goes without saying that every Ghanaian
loves food
Kenkey, fufu, banku, tuo zafi, red red and jollof
Any of these must cause your mouth to salivate
and stomach to have goosebumps

Kwer!

Eat well and never be shy of asking for seconds
You are a weapon of nutritious destruction on a
peace keeping mission for your hunger
Be proud of your stomach

The final lesson in being Ghanaian,
involves a change in behavioral mindset
It requires adopting animalistic tendencies
The art, of behaving like an ostrich
Take nonsense from no one
and be ready to kick them if they mess with you
Run whenever it is required
Towards opportunity or away from danger
And be ready to bury your head or hide in
embarrassing situations
Coming out only when the embarrassment has left
the room

Now that I am done speaking on these traits,
I will proceed to verifying if you have any of
them
Let's start with the last point
which asked you to be like an ostrich
So I ask,

How long is your neck?

YESTERDAY I DOWNLOADED LOVE

Yesterday, I downloaded love
At a speed of 10 gigabytes per second, I
downloaded love
I uninstalled a couple of applications
to make space for love
Selfishness, pride and greed are some
of the applications I uninstalled for love

Yesterday, I downloaded love
I downloaded love into my heart
Not my c drive, external drives or devices, that
are smart

Neither Windows nor Apple devices, regardless
of their hard disk space,
RAM, processor or graphics card, can manipulate
love
This is because, love does not use logic

I have been warned several times about
installing love into my soul
Some say it's a virus because it controls you
whole
Gets you to do things you did not even know
Like reconfiguring your settings and
realigning your goals

Yesterday, I downloaded love
It was free and available on all the app stores
Love is available in all languages
Compatible on all phones, tablets and operating
systems
There are no age restrictions
Though several versions exist,
the main version, is that which exists amongst
couples

Yesterday, I downloaded love
I downloaded it to connect with another person

Love is simple to use but complicated to
understand
Until you FALL in love,
you will only experience the trial version
This is similar to both Twitter and Facebook
Like Twitter, you begin by following people
With Facebook, you begin by liking persons
and accepting friend requests
Accepting many of these can make
falling in love really complicated

You can do all this in the trial version
But to experience the full power of love
you must do more than follow, like
and accept friend requests

You must fall in love

This, requires a sacrifice
Money, sex, time, commitment
and trust are a few of the currencies accepted
by love
Sacrificing these however,
does not guarantee that love would work
Not all who download and spend on love leave
happy
Some leave dead, others get pregnant
Some leave depressed or suicidal
The lucky ones, get married or divorced

Yesterday, I downloaded love

But I uninstalled it today

because...

I am broke

UNPLUGGED

I know you are thinking about me
because I am thinking about you
I miss you but I don't want to let you know
I don't want to let you go
I don't want to let you ...
Flow into my soul and hold my emotions under
arrest
for a test I repeatedly seem to fail
I fail at admiring you just for your looks
I see opportunities I am not supposed to see
Some will call it lust, I will call it...3D
A third dimensional dream
A dream that unplugs me from this world
and throws me into a fantasy
A fantasy that easily turns into reality,
with just a few buttons being pushed or a touch

You turn me into a kid dying to unlock a smart
phone
Your smart phone, which in essence is you

So what is your password? What is your pin?
And why are you pricking me with it?

You don't even try
You don't even lie
And that's the problem
You see the truth about us led us to lie in
secret,
on a bed and to ourselves

How can I forget those sweet lips that she
licked in secret?
How can I forget the silhouette of her
curvatures in the dark that passion allowed me
to see?
How can I forget the sounds she made?
Her whispers,
her folds and moans,

her bread I kneaded from her dough
How can I forget her suggestions and tell
myself
this was just ...a thing?
How can she forget my desire?
The invincible wire connecting us and causing
us to be shocked with pulses of lust,
infatuation and horniness

Maybe she can
Because before she made her bed
and stepped out to lure me into her cage of lies
and thighs
She disconnected the wire from her plug of
emotions

So she wasn't touched
That moment was fiction
I and my feelings imaginary

So here I am caught in a rendezvous with guilt
and a mirage of love
Over a girl who swept me of my feet
with a broom I can't find
A broom made of her dark chocolate lips
and ass on fire like rockets at a NASA space
station

She is heavenly and unreachable
Because she pulled the plug out of her emotions
Floated into space
And became the star that I slept with
But can never claim, as my own

AGBOGBLOSHIE

Honking, splashing, the pitter patter of the
drizzle
Honking, splashing, the pitter patter of the
drizzle
Honking, splashing, the pitter patter of the
drizzle
As a riddle of poor sounds wiggle and hijack
the Agbogbloshie market after a heavy down pour
There is dancehall in the distance as a barber's
comb and blade causes hair to fall
Destinations stick like geckos to walls
Echoes of various stops spread through the air
like calls
It's a network of confusion
The drivers never get bored

La Paz! La Paz! Circle! Circle! KoKomlemle!
Vrooooooom! Bam! Bam!

The lorry station attendant slams
the minibus like Van Damme
Waking the bank worker latching onto a few
minutes of snooze
Another is still asleep, the driver is sober
from booze
The doors scrape shut like Ayigbe's saw
massaging timber
Sawing off the option of a getaway,
the chanting of destinations,
winds by Tweduapon and birds trying to be
singers
This, is all part of the orchestra of the
Agbogbloshie market

Sssssssssss!

There is a hissing in the air rhyming with a
pissing contest
proudly sponsored by local beer

In this local brew of commotion,
resistant bleats and crowing by goats
and chickens pollute the air

Meeeeeeer!

The goats beatbox rebelliously
like provisions in a secondary school
chop box not wanting to be consumed
The chickens flap their wings aimlessly
like sisters fanning a coal pot for fire to
resume
Others are waiting for their hot porridge to
cool
The okada riders' drone through traffic
shooting
magazines of smoke and fumes
The cop is confused, caught in perfume, of
corruption dictating that the rider is a
buffoon
Having passengers without helmets,
turning safety into a joke
Hajia's Hausa koko is bubbling in a cauldron
blacker than coke
The steam from the porridge says a prayer of
hope
As it prepares for another boxing match
with the colors of smoke, or carbon monoxide
The frogs and cockroaches sit as referees for
offside
The bubbles in Daavi's cauldron are in a similar
fight
with the black, green bubbles in a cinema typed,
the soupy gutter

The documentary is about to start
Quack! Quack!

The real ugly duckling is paddling through a
river of back-packs, car batteries, plastic
bags, bottles and borla

Rubbish and chaos fight like buyers and sellers
haggling not over price but who is taller
In this bassa bassa party,
it's interesting how Christianity finds a coat
to wear
Heaven seems unavailable in this market where
all swear
The roadside preacher thunders with his Bible
and Mjolnir
His microphone, to ensure that the truth is now
heard

"Praise the Lord!"

Says the preacher in suit and tie
Sweat falls from his face like a criminal about
to die
He pauses to wipe his forehead
Counting the coins, the crowds denies
Grateful for the blessings he sees as God's
reply

Kwasia!

Twi insults and slaps flow
Between Fatima and Hajia over a customer who
throws
10 cedis as tip
They both made the trip
but alas there is no change for the money to be
split

Passersby and the stench of rottenness refuse
to turn
Mary is going over the juju she fears
She recalls the instructions about the
eye shadow and lip balm
By the time the sky's turn dark
John, her soon to be lover, will be in her arms

Bzzzzzzzzzzzzz!

Olu the Ga fly buzzes over with his family
It's a day out to experience a good meal and
tragedy
They spot a dead dog and feast on the insanity
Thanking the chef, Agbogbloshie, for satisfying
their vanity

Time however turns differently for Adjorkor's
spatula
in her dadesɛn
Happiness and pain wedded here
but still quarrel in anansesɛm
Sodom and Gomorrah pollute
and corrupt for the title of king
The committee of vultures
is comfortable in this heaven of things
Everyone in the market is hungry
Looking for a better life
Opportunity is still single
Looking for a better wife
But Agbogbloshie is toxic
Demand and supply his thugs
Turning the wheels of profit
into a land of drugs

So I am a Pinocchio in Ghana
Standing on a rubbish hill
Saying that things will be better
Yet my nose catch Lavender hill

Poet's Notes

My experience with Agbogbloshie is a story that came about because of a girl I was interested in (who eventually became my wife). She worked at a financial institution at Agbogbloshie and I would sometimes drop her off for work or pick her up.

Agbogbloshie is a market, scrap yard, dumping site and home to several Ghanaians in the lower brackets. Despite its grim appearance it's a commercial hub for a lot of business. The scenery is a collage of beauty, confusion and hope.

I used to sit in the car and watch what was going on around me whenever I came into the area. There was always something interesting to see and write about.

VANISH

The last time I saw Vanessa,
she seemed to vanish effortlessly
She must have been playing the game hide and
seek
on an expert level
Finding her name was a treasure hunt without a
map
And though we were on the same campus,
I seemed to find and loose her
like a baby playing with a marble
Eventually, the vanishing effect wore off
I don't know whether it was her dimple
or the dress she wore
But something about Vanessa that evening,
led me to explore the possibility of us being
intimate
My advances were innocent
I assumed and believed that she wanted what I
wanted
But what did I want?

Friendship?
Or the taste of her lips?

She was different
Something about her sentences on life had
purpose
She looked into my eyes and saw more of me
than anyone in my family ever saw
I admit, she may have been drunk on love
and the cell phone units I purchased for her
But it was a deserving feeling
I guess we were…in love
Everything about the way we did things felt
electric
Whether we held hands, hugged or were afar,
It felt as if we tingled
As if we itched to be closer

Bonding like chemicals to form solutions to
diseases
Ours was loneliness with a twist of horny
The night that we bonded
was everything a couple in love would have
wanted
I liken it to the R-rated version of Aladdin
if after the magic carpet ride with Jasmine,
Aladdin crept in
Words wouldn't do justice to how our bodies
spoke
Our hands, legs and waist,
communicated and danced exquisitely
Praising and reveling, in ecstasy and unison

As beautiful as that moment was,
none of us were thinking about a baby
So when Vanessa told me she was pregnant,
I played back our love scene looking for the
point where I became stupid and reckless enough
to not have protected myself
The fault was mine - and hers
But that is water under the bridge
Or should I say, in her belly

Our romance quickly transformed into a blame
game
None of us were ready for the responsibility of
being parents
I questioned my feelings towards her
Where was the electricity that we felt before?
Or did the shock of the pregnancy create a
surge that prevented our circuits from working
I tried to justify her as wife material but
came up short
I don't think I was husband or father material
either
A bad drinking habit, betting on soccer,
clubbing and a lack of church and a job
were not traits a woman looked for in a husband
or father

I thought time will make things better
I often hoped to wake up from the weird wet
nightmare But reality had other plans
We still hadn't told our parents
Just a close friend or two who kept
questioning what our next move was
An abortion looked like the way out
I was afraid to suggest it,
as another argument wouldn't make the baby
vanish

Was the child even mine?
Another question I didn't have evidence to
justify
The torment was more than my itchiness
to taste her lips before

Eventually, I gave in
I resolved to do the right thing and stand by
her
We discussed and even shared a kiss
Electricity begun to flow again
But something was wrong
She suddenly felt violated internally
She froze and was scared
Quickly, she asked that I rush her to a
hospital
I deduced that it had to do with the baby
I was however more worried about her
In the car, she kept yelling for the driver to
hurry
I felt weak and useless
Unable to help in any way but urge the driver
along with her to move as fast as he could

At the hospital, she was rushed into the
emergency ward
I moved about and sat repeatedly,
worrying about a million things including her
life,

the child, her parents and what the bill
of the treatment will cost

Again, I felt useless
I realized the weakness of man
I wish I could take her pain, share in it to a
degree to contemplate what she was going
through
But that was not my destiny

After what seemed like forever,
The nurse called for me to see the doctor
who after interrogating me like a headmaster,
proceeded to inform me about the miscarriage
Hours ago, this is what I wanted

Not exactly

I just wished the baby would vanish

Is vanishing this painful?

Is there a way to undo it?

I wonder whether my thoughts turned into a
prayer

Is this my opportunity to say amen?

I felt lost, hurt and inefficient
As I walked to her bed to break the news to her
I couldn't help but wonder whether my intention
and the fruit of my labor, were different

All I wanted was to touch her lips

I ended up giving her a baby
and taking it away at the same time

I took her to heaven and to hell

How is she still alive?

What power is this that causes such joy and
grief?

If vanishing is this painful, tell me

Why haven't I disappeared yet?

OUR GUTTERS

Our gutters are tunnels of revelation
Rabbit holes like that of Alice in wonderland
but with a foul smell, green juice, urine and
plastic
Down here we collect rain and piss
We wish, they possessed the disappearing
ability
of recycle bins on our computers but often, we
miss
When we throw garbage into them
practicing a free throw at a basketball game
It's a crying shame
Our gutters are death traps
with their own personal problems
Like the economy, they are convoluted
Their purpose has been dissected
and repurposed illegally to act both as a sewer
and land fill
Our gutters want poodles and chihuahuas
as pets and not rats and mice
They are sick of cockroaches and mosquitoes
and are tired of taking shit
Our gutters are millennials
tired of giving birth to more gutters
for them to be enslaved and abused
They are tired of being premature adoption
centers
for aborted children and fetuses in bloom
They are tired of being left out of the smoking
chain
Receiving leftover smoked out cigarette butts
and not the full thing
Our gutters want money
and not rubbish thrown into them
They too want to live a life of luxury
They want clean water to flow through
A bit of light, electricity and air
conditioners

On occasion, a vehicle is given to a gutter
during a flood
This is really a coffin
and not something that the gutter can use
As a dead driver and passengers
are usually occupying the machines
Our gutters are mirrors into our lifestyle
A dark hole of truth about our shady dealings
Lies are converted into truth down here
The owners seldom come for them
Down here the gutter is a weird strip club
customer
Disgusted and excited about viewing vaginas and
penises by willing parties willing to free
themselves from piss
Our gutters are drug addicts indulging in coke,
heroin, antibiotics and anything one can sniff
It however does little to numb the pain they
feel
They harbor condoms and sperm
Yet can't protect themselves from diseases
or give birth to children unless an egg is
provided
Our gutters are jumped over and crossed
Neglected, afflicted and considered unimportant
like snot Just like the human treating life
Our gutters are a disgusting reflection of us
No matter the effort we use to clean it
It will forever remain revolting and unaccepted
Precious water bodies
are being converted into a religion of gutters
and we don't seem to care
There are many disciples flowing in repugnance
and promising freedom at a fare
How did the river become the gutter in the
alley?
How did the pond become choked with plastic?
How did the stream loose its magic?
Water body called human
I ask you these questions
Why aren't you chasing waterfalls?

Why are you chasing rejected waste
and keeping yourself beneath the sun?
Why are you choosing to be a gutter and not the
oasis?
Why are you not choosing greatness?
Settling for the filtered waste of the world?

Why?

And here, we wait for the answer
But it is prevented from passing through
It has been blocked in a gutter
by things that were once answers too
Answers tired of being mistreated
Answers tired of being used
Answers tired of being repeated
To the question, "who are you?"

STONES

Let's play stones
Let's run around chasing each other
throwing little rocks at our skin and bones
I know you will dodge skillfully
So throw well
Make the game fun
No slow throws
Just fast, rotating, hard chips
Spinning like ninja weapons
You are a Ghanaian ninja in chale wote
attacking deadly assassins
who just plundered your village and belongings

Who is on my team?

You over there look like a strong team player
with skill
The look in your eye when you threw that stone
at the lizard says it all

Come join me

Let's conquer and take over the nations
The stones on the park
that the Pentecost Church is using
to build its church is all the ammunition
we need for this adventure

Girls are welcome to join

It's stones after all
It's not dangerous
Just looks it

The aim is to make it look real
We really don't want to see blood gushing from
our frenemies skin
Or a swollen forehead
His head is already big

We however expect to get dirty
Dust and mud with a few scratches and sand in
our hair

Nothing a good bath by mother wouldn't fix

The dogs will have a field day
They can run with us
But don't let any adult see you
They are sure to put this glorious fire of a
game out cold

The park is ours and the stones are free

Let's celebrate our childhood
Before we grow old
And start throwing real stones, at each other

Poet's Notes

I attended a funeral at a church and found kids
playing with stones on the church grounds. They
were throwing gravel from a heap that was going
to be used to complete ongoing construction in
the church. The park was pretty large, so they
had enough space to run and distance between
each other to throw. The danger and fun mixed
with nostalgia of my own childhood, prompted me
to write this poem.

THE DETOUR

We have a complicated relationship, but it is
sexy
I should have put a ring on your finger before
we said the,
three words, two nouns, one verb,
I heard, we were to wed before you
moved into my house
But you had the next-door neighbor kind of
beauty
The kinda' cutie, that viewed me as a casanova
A cassava provider with a potential to own a
Range Rover
I mean we had fifty shades of brown sugar
The house was Nestle
You were Milo, I was Nido
We made hot chocolate and made me purchase a
tuxedo
Because I thought I was more than your hero
But there was never a wedding gown
Just a lot of town
A lot of time wasting, window shopping,
booty hopping, and she had! The booty
But why did I buy the suit before the ring?
How did I make her a spouse without the string,
of commitment?
I guess I got carried away
Her beauty blinded my destiny and caused me to
detour
This was a seesaw
A nice adventure, but not life
She is a girl for the sheets, but not for a wife
And I am ready to move on
Break whatever this thing is and continue my
life
But that morning she wore a dress
A wonderful silk robe which she wore as a
present
My weakness grew stronger and broke my defenses
as she bent over and asked me to detour again

Lorgorligi Locomotion   Hondred Percent

and again, and again

I KNOW YOUR SOUND

I know your sound
You are a blue colored note mixed with hues of
green dancing with the strings of the ocean
The waves are in constant praise of your beauty

The sea invites you for a swim with the sun
The warm bath nourishes your tones
The liquids oil the nectar of your sound
Your toes find the hidden strings of the kora
beneath the ground,
Plucking footsteps of a sonata
Your ankles and hips sizzle the maracas
Beads and cowries adorned on your curves,
gyrate to the African rhythm within

Your djembe heart is lined with the hide of
prized game
Your beats are poised with authority and fame
Your presence is strikingly undeniable

Look at your arms
Slender and strong like the bamboo
Your piercings allow the wind to flow with your
canoe
Through your atɛntɛben body

You are nourishing like shampoo
Through you we hear songs of hope,
and songs of taboos

Your breasts and buttocks are both guitars
One however is electric
The other, plays the bass
I would leave your imagination,
to decide who is the bass
Look out for vibrations,
it should help solve the case

Now bless me with a symphony

257

Bless me, with a song
Move my heart to understand you
Move my heart to belong
You are spectacle to behold
A moving masterpiece, untold
Now that I have found you,
I'm never going home

Tell your mother that I listened
That I listened to your soul
There I found truth
and heard justice propose

I became a criminal
Your song I stole
For love to arrest,
and cuff me to your soul

I WANT TO FALL DOWN SOME

It starts with the Lord's Prayer
Morning devotion followed by Psalm 23
I have been on this path of Christianity
from birth till 23, and yet,
I have not fallen down some
I come to the church every Sunday
Participate in all weekly activities
I jump, dance and shout higher than any
congregation member during praise and worship
I admit, I don't pray in tongues,
but lead Sunday-school and form part of the
choir
I am what you call a chrifay guy who lives life
and does everything by the book, and yet,
I have not fallen down some
Even Fiifi has fallen down some
How is that possible?
Fiifi, the womanizer, who apparently
gave his life to Christ two weeks ago,
fell under the anointing just this Wednesday

What a shock!

Abena, the girl who I know
has slept with all the bad boys on campus,
even has fallen down some
Even my sister has fallen,
and I am badder than her
So why hasn't the Lord caused my fall?

Do I come late for the service?
Is my height the issue?
Should I barber my hair santo
for the oil to activate the vibrations
properly?
Is it because I am not faithful with my tithe?
or give only 5 GHC as offering?
What am I doing wrong?

Look, I have tried sitting at different places
Just to catch the anointing
Some nights I scream Hallelujah!
Other nights, I sit quiet

Did this increase my chances
of my head touching the floor? No!

I just want to fall down!
My relationship with God
is at the brink of extinction
because of this automatic holy gesture,
that has little or nothing to do with gravity

Some of you listening to this rant
may be saying to yourselves,

"But it's not everyone who falls down"

It's not everyone too who goes to university
Are you saying that I am not special?
Speak for yourself
Sometimes when the man of God is passing by,
I feel the electricity going through me
I believe I am about to fall down
and open my eyes only to see
the man of God on the other side
At those embarrassing moments,
I am glad to be in a prayer service
where majority have their eyes closed

But what do I think will happen when I fall
down?

Will Jesus speak to me?
Will I travel instantaneously to Heaven
to drink with the Apostles for 30 minutes
to an hour and come back to life?
Will I simply have a vision?
Or like Bukom Banku descending after a right
hook punch, will my face just hit the floor?

I can't say I have thought about the experience
much
I have been so caught up in the hype of falling,
that I have never really questioned
what happens during and after the fall

What if, I am just afraid of falling down?
Our church after all is not covered with
pillows or carpets
I don't think tiled floors make for a soft
landing

And do I fall forwards or backwards?
How about sideways?
I have never seen a sideways fall before
Is that an illegal fall?
Is there such a thing?
Has anyone died or been hurt from falling?
None that I am aware of
Either the angels or ushers will catch you
Do churches have insurance for that?
I don't think so
I guess having insurance makes
the whole falling down affair fake
But it's such risky business
Every time I am touched by a man of God,
I am always thinking about my fall
If any descent happens it feels, unholy,
normal, gravity induced

Where is the lightning?
The thunder and smoke?
The flashes, lights and earthquakes only I will
hear?
Why am I also expecting such
a chaotic extravaganza to occur?

I don't know

But tomorrow during service

I am going to walk to the man of God
and ask for prayers

During the prayers,
as he lays his hands on me,
insurance or no insurance,
I am trusting God, the angels and the ushers,

(in that specific order)

and falling down

This time,
I won't resist the man of God's … push

Poet's Notes

As a Christian in Ghana, one is bound to have experienced the falling down scenario. For those who don't know what this is, this is when people in church come under the anointing a fall.

Some of it is genuine and some...debatable.

I have seen it numerous times and had been involved in many conversations on the matter. This poem is inspired by a conversation with a man who got pissed at a man of God for not touching him during a weeklong evening service. All he wanted was to be touched and he did not understand why he was being ignored. The other is an experience my brother had with a pastor when we were kids and how he intentionally resisted being pushed by the man when being prayed for.

HOW TO STEAL MEAT FROM A POT

Good morning fellow stealers
Today we are going to go through
some vital life skills to survive
the innocence test conducted by mothers,
aunts and cookers of soup
The mission,
is to steal meat from soup

Follow these instructions carefully
if you want to be successful in satisfying
your carnivorous cravings

Look left and right to see if somebody is
coming
Move silently and remember that you are
stealing
You'll ask for forgiveness after the deed is
done
Check the position of the ladle
Remember how you met it to secure your
innocence
As you open the pot, make sure not to drop the
cover
Use a napkin to ensure that you do this without
burning your hand and ruining the operation

Count the meat inside the pot with the ladle
Use a napkin or gloves whilst doing this to
prevent fingerprints being used as evidence to
track you down
Remember, the suspects are only those in your
household
The number to remember when counting the meat,
is 5
If the meat is 5 or more, take one
If it is less, just bite what you want
Use your teeth and take the meat on a sliming
course
Bite small, not big

The meat has to look countable and
inconspicuous
Now cover the pot slowly
Throughout the operation,
listen out for footsteps
Place an obstacle along the path to the kitchen
to alert you when someone is coming
to give you enough time to cover your tracks
A baby's rattle, empty tin or noisy pair of
slippers would do

Under no circumstances shall the soup
stain your clothes or touch anything in the
kitchen
If it stains the kitchen floor,
clean up quickly, with an excuse in hand
if someone walks in
If your clothes get stained,
rush to the bathroom and dab some soap
to wash out the stain and change your attire
The evidence must be dealt with

If gloves are not used for the operation,
wash your hands
Wash your hands with soap and apply sanitizer
with a minimum of 80% alcohol to eliminate the
smell

Now pop gum into your mouth to kill odor
If gum is not available,
brush your teeth twice for five minutes
Now leave the kitchen like an angel
leaving the sanctuary of the most high

Tomorrow we'll learn how to steal a boyfriend or
girlfriend
Those in relationships are forbidden to attend
We want to have a group discussion afterward
and I don't want to see practical's occurring
during the discussion
Class dismissed

Poet's Notes

My son once stole meat from a pot of soup with a lot of evidence on his t-shirt. This led to a good spanking by his mom which had me laughing at his amateur thievery.

Stealing meat from a pot is something that kids do from time to time. I decided to thus provide some friendly advice for my son's next attempt to be successful.

This was inspired by a social media post.

DESIRE

I had a certain desire for Greek yogurt
Greek yogurt and granola mixed with
raisins and sprinkled cinnamon
Greek yogurt and granola mixed with raisins,
sprinkled cinnamon, raspberries, cherries and
honey

My desire had created the perfect dessert
and deserted me to a utopia of bliss
The bowl holding this scrumptious delight
was made of ivory
The silver spoon, with gold highlights
enriched the taste of the rainbow of flavors
within
My smile at this beauty shrunk to sadness as my
eyes awoke from this surreal imagination

I had to lick that vanilla flavored yogurt
Probably suck a strawberry if my money would
allow
It was the perfect excuse to take a trip to the
grocery store
A trip to bore the aisles with the chords of
desire
playing on my emotions

I deserved that promotion

In minutes, I had arrived
Shopping like Paris Hilton for a new wardrobe
Stilettos were bananas, diamonds were cherries
and perfume were cinnamon
All that was left was the yogurt
I stepped up to the fridge and slid the glass
door
I was about to pick the object of my desire
Immediately, it felt as if I had opened
pandora's box

Simultaneously as I grabbed the yoghurt,
I felt my skirt behind me lift
A cold chiseled palm invaded my thighs
Caressing the right cheek of my buttocks

I froze

Not because I was in the cold area
Something about the unexpected,
especially, in a supposedly public setting
activates a scary pause button

Every stroke of his promiscuous palm on me
gripped me with increased fear, and turned me
into a snail
Slowing down my thoughts and movements
Coiling me into an ugly shell of shame

When he was done,
he smacked my behind like I was his bitch
Like a good dog, I whimpered silently in my pain
My eyes immediately popped out in shock
My spine popped upright ninety degrees in a
jump that saw me clench by ass

After a few seconds,
When I felt it was safe

I began to breathe

I crawled out of my shell of shame
and turned my head to view my defiler
I had other items to pick up
I however instinctively sped towards
the checkout counter to pay and exit
And there he was
Beaming with a smile
Our eyes met and he gave me a wink
Stroking his manhood awaiting his turn to pay
He was confident I wasn't going to say a thing
And he was right

At my admission in thought,
I left my basket
Walked briskly to my car
and drove home to sink into my bed

I cried

I cried not because I could not have my Greek
yogurt,
the object of my desire
But because
I had become his object of desire
Without my permission he stole my confidence
Stole my confidence and dignity, turning me
from a victim
into a shameful excuse for Greek yoghurt
He turned me into Greek yoghurt without flavor
Without cherries, raspberries, raisins, cinnamon
and honey

He turned me,

into nothing

Poet's Notes

I remember listening to a program on BBC about
a lady in Egypt who got groped at a grocery
store. The description of her emotions and
helplessness, alongside other stories of
similar instances, led me to write this poem to
bring light to the abuse that some see as play.

These are serious issues that are being
trivialized. Let us add our voices to the
discussion in the best way we know how.

A LONG CAUSE OF DEATH NOTICE

You left us no choice
You entered our home illegally
Scared my wife and had us turning
our kitchen upside down
You then took the liberty of inviting more
friends over
An argument ensued about
how you made it into the house
The evidence was clear in the morning
It was through the window
The police were contacted
Preliminary investigations revealed a break in
Suspects were however nowhere to be found
The police advised us to keep doors
locked and lay a trap to catch you
I assumed the worst was over
Days later, close to midnight in the hall
You crept up on me
Gave me a fright and hid
I knew you meant no harm, so wanted to let you
go
But you were stupid and stubborn
You kept shifting your hiding place
You left me no choice
So, I called the police again
After a long game of hide and seek that lasted
till morning
We snuffed you out and killed you
Your accomplice was found the next day
in the kitchen under the stove
Dead from poison
Smelling like the havoc you both wrecked upon
us
May this extensive cause of death notice,
serve as a warning to all mice in the area
Kaa ba enshia

KWAKWE LAST STOP

Look at what they did to my brothers
These hypocrites love and celebrate
us on their flat screens
Yet when we come into their home,
They kill us

This wasn't the plan!

What's up, Disney World?
I think Mickey and Minnie are slacking off on
the job
We are supposed to be loved, cuddled and fed
Everyone loves Jerry mouse more than Thomas the
cat
So why are we not made welcome in your
households?
Look at the role models I just mentioned
And let's not forget Mighty Mouse, Speedy
Gonzalez and the courageous Reepicheep in the
C.S. Lewis classic, Chronicles of Narnia

Alas, no mouse in Ghana has inspired us enough
We don't want cheese, wɔ sumɔ kenkey
Kena bibioo kɛ sardines too, won't be bad
We too are affected by hardships
and feel the heat of the economic sun

We were here first
We lived happily in the open field,
till some real estate developers
came and built these houses

Where do you want us to go?
Nɛɛ gbɛ o sumɔ ni wɔ ya?
You took our home and when we come for a visit,
you kill us
Mɛni sane po nɛ?
How much at all can a mouse eat?
And where will a mouse go?

In my short life here on earth
I have come to realize, that we are not
respected by humans
They often confuse us with rats
Buuluuanii!
Such an abomination!
We are different
Much cuter, and less disgusting

My brothers and sisters
These are dark times
Kaa fee dull!
We fight the cat and his owner
Loving Ewes for killing and eating our enemy
Let's bear in mind these dangers we face
and walk the earth dying proud mice
Fighting for Ewes and all cat eaters,
to gain, political control

Poet's Notes

The poem follows through from the previous
piece which narrated a real event that happened
in my house. We had a mouse enter our house and
give my family and I a fright leading to an all-
out war against the rodent at midnight.

We took all our furniture out trying to get
this mouse out of the house. The mouse ended up
hiding in an old gas cooker which we blocked
off until the morning.

Once the sun was up, we took the cooker outside
and looked for the mouse with no luck. There
were suggestions that this villain had escaped.

It was still in the cooker, and we eventually
flushed it out and killed it. The whole
experience took my creative mind down this path
of feeling sorry for the mouse and personifying
the experience from his family's point of view.

JESUS PIECE

If love fails, at least I got my Jesus piece
Piece of God made with plastic,
a needless piece
I pray to God to give us all some
Jesus peace, a piece of love
but he has been knocking
for at least three weeks

Times up,

hope you all have some Jesus peace

They say heaven is a place
where all the Christians meet
What's a Christian?
My bad, I thought they live discreet
Not all who go to Church believes He speaks
Forgive these peeps
Not all church goers are at least this deep

We come to church but sin
for the sin too sweet
Play the game of go to hell
with conviction see
We instantly point fingers with religious
speech
or thoughts of course
No plank on my eye I thought
So didn't see hypocrisy coming on board
Becoming captain of this boat
which is a hoax but pause
With a connection to this deception
I create a ship on tour
called relationship
Sin is the anchor on this baby, quick!
Give me the fruit so I can
bite and see reality shift

And blame you and not me

My future is unseen
I try to come clean
but without grace I am unseen

My heart seeks God, yet seeks the obscene
Matthew 6:6, Lord I want to believe

So I hang your son around my neck
to change my dreams
But don't have him in my heart
So my life's unclean

At least I look good
Tell those coming up to look hood
Good don't buy enough food
to make you look cool around here
Our battery is not love it's all fear
The battle is for survival
The main plan is, "I don't care"

You see I am trying to see
tomorrow with my family

The key to that door sometimes
means dancing with insanity

Gravity is fictional,
but sin holds you to the ground
They say Jesus is the way,
but this way I have not found

So I act tough, mad bluff
I am looking for peace
It's all locked
The path I am on won't get me there
You see I am chicken I got smallpox
But need God

Or more specifically, I need Jah!
The weed told me and pointed
to a clean serene jar

A vision of the son of man
on a cross with clean hands
Pierced like a criminal
All to clean man

That had me thinking...
Why him and not we?
We messed up the carpet
We made it unclean

They say that's the price of sin
I am in thought with a glass of gin
Holding my Jesus piece
like a phone to a card of sim
Knowing there is truth
to this Christianity
I'm thirsty
but the Christians are not giving me clarity

I guess I am inadequate
Not perfect a good addict sick,
on life and its pleasures
At least I am honest and not a graduate

But I need strength
Some of what that dude on the cross has
In the school of life,
that right there is a hall pass
Next level peace
And I want three full bags
So I lean on him to disappear,
and not feel too bad

That's the trick to being found
The trick to being sound
loose yourself in pain and what is known as
fickle bounds
of anger
Until you find the hidden sound
Which is love and prosperity

Bound in a little file,
called humility

But you have to lose yourself

To access this immunity
you must lose your wealth

Lose your heart
Your desires
You must lose your stealth
Trade your invincibility cloak
In order to renew your health
And find peace

If love fails
at least I got my Jesus piece
Piece of God made with plastic,
a needless piece
I pray to God to give us all
some Jesus peace
A piece of love, but he has been knocking for at
least three weeks

Times up,

Hope you all have some Jesus peace

IF WESTERN SUPERHEROES LIVED IN GHANA AND NAIJA

If superheroes were in Ghana and Nigeria
Spiderman would be begging Nigerians to calm
down after breaking his 12th electricity pole

Deadpool would be swearing in English and Igbo
at Nigerian tailors for not sewing his costume
after two months

Batman would never exist
His uncle would have claimed his father's
inheritance

If that didn't happen,
Batman would have pastors
and villagers as his villains,
Cursing and casting out the devil
in him for being a grand wizard

The Flash would relocate to Ghana after
discovering real traffic in Lagos

Cyborg and Tony Stark will be
frustrated with dumsor after hours
of no electricity to charge their suits

If superheroes were in Ghana,
Wonder Woman will save Auntie Comfort
from a vehicle at Agbogbloshie market
and receive thanks and scolding
from her for wearing a short skirt

"Why are you dressed like an ashawo?"

Disappointed, she will hop to Naija
in a single bound to have her lasso of truth
around Ibrahim at Yaba market
Querying him on why he groped her behind
Beast Boy at this time will be
bleating and begging Okoye

279

not to sell him for suya
after turning into a ram

Spiderman would realize that commuting
via swinging is restricted to Airport City in
Ghana as Accra lacks skyscrapers to swing from

Bruce Wayne will question becoming a superhero
as he realizes that throwing cash works as well
as batarangs in defeating enemies

Robin in assisting with traffic
will save a pedestrian with the left hand
and get the response,

"I can see you don't have respect"

If superheroes were in Ghana and Nigeria,
Cyborg would save Mary from armed robbers, and
Mary would be asking if he has a USB port to
charge her phone

Boys from Abosseyokai and Aba
will be looking for means to steal
spare parts from Cyborg
when he is defeated by villains

Captain America would be renamed
Captain Kumerika
and would awake one morning in Kumasi
to find his shield being used to fry kelewele

Spiderman would quit his job
after realizing that the only thing
he is good for is to dance
at children's parties
His new adversary on the party scene
is Mickey Mouse

Clark Kent AKA Superman
would be caught in a dilemma

between being a journalist or a contractor when
he finds that he can make 2K daily
from carrying blocks and cements at sites

Martian Manhunter would question his powers
when he sees slay queens shape shifting with
waist trainers and make up

Sango worshippers and Voltarians
will be in awe after seeing Thor
summon thunder without incantations

Loki will be an MP
profiting illegally from state funds
A pastor of a mega church, and
President of the Fraud Boys Association,
due to his mastery in deception

Superman will come to Benin
and the Eastern region of Ghana and realize,
that he is not the only human that can fly

If superheroes were in Ghana and Nigeria, Hulk
would have alone dealt with
the Boko Haram militia

Aqua Man would have caught
all those involved with galamsey

The Joker and The Punisher
will team up to end SARS

Harley Quinn, Cat Woman and Poison Ivy,
will be prominent female gang leaders
Cat Woman specifically,
will have a love hate relationship
with Ewe men

Black Panther and Blade
will be friends and celebrities in Nollywood
always arguing about who is the coolest

Most however, would have ended up like Hancock,
The Homelander or Omniman
Drunk on drugs, booze, corruption and power

If superheroes were in Ghana and Nigeria,
I don't think much will change
For corruption is celebrated
And heroism, seen as strange

I MISS THE ARGUMENTS

She sits there by the fancy vase
Eyeballs of "why me?" and regret stuck in an
angry face

Her stomach is filled with food,
but her heart has a hungry plate
Cranky, she looks around searching for hope in
the ugly place

Everything is not beautiful
So she's mad like it's her monthly take,
on her period

But it's John

And John is not gone

He is somewhere other than here,
but she wants John to be gone

For its long and irritating
to be waiting for John to change his response,
to her demands

She wants John to be mad

Mad at the situation
But John is not the bad
John is not the dragon barking angry type

He is the,
"everything will be okay, just chill",
the cool annoying type,
who just wants peace

She also wants peace
Just thinks the road he is on will bring water
and not peace, to her eyes
The bartender looks at her all surprised

I had a wife once, he said
And she pissed me off!
She made these fried eggs with onions in the
morning which I never liked
Every morning we would argue about it
Not the eggs in particular
but the onions
She said it was good for me
because of my blood pressure

I am talking World War 2
kind of arguments with
F-bombs and shit grenades
all because I had a minor stroke once

And she will hit me

Not like Tyson but,
little painless punches
that would piss me off

You know how you women do?

She would call me ungrateful,
bring up my exes and stuff in the past
that's unnecessary

Funny enough I believe this
made my blood pressure rise
I bet the damn onions in the eggs were why I
didn't get a heart attack

This happened every single day
It was crazy I tell you
But not as crazy as when she passed

She died last Christmas in a car accident

As irritating as she was,
not a day goes by where
I don't wish her irritating sexy

ass was around

Of all the things I miss about that lady
what I miss most was those onion arguments
I even wish they would be longer
I now fry my eggs with onions,
not because I like them or the health benefits

But I want to

I want to get pissed off at God and have similar
arguments with Him but....
He is not exactly the talking back type

Plus, it feels awkward
But I still do it

It gives me a certain level of comfort
Not quite the comfort I desire but you get the
idea

So, I hear what you are saying about
cool and annoying John
I get why it's irritating, I really do
What I am telling you to do is to embrace it
Because from the story you told me,
that man is not hitting you
or sleeping around
He is not perfect,
but you will miss annoying John
when he is gone
Just accept him and survive

I wish I did that
I wish I accepted and cherished that annoying
woman everyday she was around
And I advise you do the same
I would do anything to get into a silly onion
argument with her
Anything to look at her pissed off face calling
me ungrateful and hitting me

For that was her way
of telling me that she loved me
And these days,

I don't hear her voice anymore

Poet's Notes

This poem is inspired by a conversation between
Frank Castle AKA the Punisher and Karen Page in
a diner in Daredevil season 2 episode 11 - .380.

The conversation is about Karen complaining
about Mat Murdock as a love interest and Frank
envying her for having a love interest to be
mad about.

I am a big Marvel and DC fan and find the
dialogue that occurs between the characters
fascinating.

LOGOLOGO LINE

Life is one loooooooong logologo line

A logologo line with logoligi vibes
with rain drops of lovi lovi

Odorlicious moments of spiced bofloats
and ripe words to sweeten the
curves of the threads of love

A tug of war of culture and the west,
Amerley and her chest,
of treasure that causes my forehead to salivate
with sweat at the prospects of a squeeze

Today it's logologo
Tomorrow logoligi

Like the tides,
the twists and turns off life are unpredictable

Life wears a disguise of calm,
but proves to be a troublesome dancer when
dancing agbadza beneath the surface

How do we dance with such a storm?

Do I tickle thunder? Or blind lightning?
Kiss electricity if you dare,
you go chop more than logoligi sensations deep
in your spine
You may find yourself in bed in a coffin with
the obituary notice

"What a shock!"

Indeed, this journey is filled with
shocks, blocks, cocks
crowing and waking us up to the logolations of
life and its true color

What is the color of life?
Black and white or red, red?
Sometimes it's a blue film screwing with your
mind just for immoral pleasure

Sometimes things are basaaaa for a time before
the sun go kai your face
And when she remembers,
it's not a guarantee that her cousin luck will
shine in your direction

It's what we call a logolity
A rickety, lickety, symphony
bound in mystery
A journey of obolobo pride becoming a
lengelenge blow man,
fighting and pushing the logologo agenda

It sounds funny and at moments
e no dey make sense
Yet we strive to comprehend the ligilities of
the sagacious philosopher called life

There is no telling where this wind will blow
The compass is forever spinning,
and today it may snow
Such are the waters of tomorrow
A guessing game famous for potential
and danger
Waters that will take you towards opportunity
and yet can sink your desires
It's the same for all
A monologue continuing to draw the logologo
Bending the logoligi with laughter and tears
Till the logs in the logologo forest,
cease to exist

Poet's Notes

I bend the rules of grammar to form several words. Some are created in this piece to spice the poem. Odorlicious is a word I coined back in the day whilst I was dating my wife. A misspelled term if we are being technical. The word ɔdɔ (odor), means love in Twi. ɔdɔlicious, is a word describing the delicious nature of love.

Logolations, is simply a self-imposed synonym of revelations but using the word logologo to describe its unexpected nature.

Ligilities, is another word for legalities.

Obolobo is the local twi word for fat person.

Lengelenge is the opposite and means skinny.

Lovi Lovi is slang for romance and "basaaa" simply means, messed up.

Logologo is derived from the word, homologous.

Logoligi however, is the description of worm like or winding movement. I hope I have unraveled the logoligi into a homologous line.